FOLLOWING BREADCRUMBS

FOLLOWING BREADCRUMBS

TALES OF A ROCK AND ROLL GIRL CHILD

JAMIE JOHNSTON

iUniverse®

FOLLOWING BREADCRUMBS
TALES OF A ROCK AND ROLL GIRL CHILD

iUniverse books may be ordered through booksellers or by contacting:

iUniverse
1663 Liberty Drive
Bloomington, IN 47403
www.iuniverse.com
1-800-Authors (1-800-288-4677)

ISBN: 978-1-5320-2926-4 (sc)
ISBN: 978-1-5320-2927-1 (e)

Library of Congress Control Number: 2017911820

Print information available on the last page.

iUniverse rev. date: 08/11/2017

'Following Breadcrumbs' refers to the process by which any of us who have followed a dream, will look to those who have traveled that path before. Then, if we are fortunate enough to have achieved that dream, and then experience a great fall from grace—we may spend the rest of our lives following our own breadcrumbs, trying to re-create in some form, the circumstances that brought us to that first triumph.

Most of us never find it again.

For Gene and Don

Contents

INTRO

I don't know what happened. This started out as a coming of age story and here it ends up practically a goddamn love story for the ages. I didn't want to write this kind of stuff. There are so many writers who do it better. My forte is pop culture—pop music, anything that goes pop, except maybe the Boston Pops.

I mean, I was a Hollywood movie star brat and a rock and roll girl child growing up in Los Angeles, the film and music industry's ground zero. Surely there would be enough crazy stories of 6 degrees of separation to fill a tome on that. I didn't need to get all hearts and flowers on everybody, did I? Just because I happened to fall in love with a few people—all of whom left indelible marks etched forever onto my heart and soul, two of whom happened to die on me, leaving me here to stew in my own haunted puddle of regrets and shoulda couldas.

But alas, at the risk of sounding sexist, that's what happens when you mix rock music and females, it can get emotional. I am a prime example. Even at my most jaded and cynical, I would cry at Lassie movies. "E.T., phone home?" Oh, I'm a goner every time. And play me the "Bookends Theme" from Simon and Garfunkel and I'm ready for the straitjacket. Seriously.

There are those in my life that will find some of what lies herein as quite a shock. Sorry about that. But I've always been a truth junkie, this isn't new. I've never suffered phonies or bull shitters well, least of all when I bullshitted myself, so I just had to back up and stop. It was time to face whatever demons lay in wait for me, the ones barely visible out of the corner of my eye, slithering silently, just under the surface of my awareness. Indeed, I have the Scorpio affliction of compartmentalizing parts of myself so that one part doesn't recognize the other. I can harbor a secret obviously—or at least hide it long enough till it wears out its welcome on my psyche and bores a hole into me so deep, I pour out onto the floor like a Salvador Dali painting. That is apparently what happened to me in the summer of 2011. I had a bit of a meltdown you could say. A bit.

So now I'm taking myself to a cheap alternative to psychotherapy. It's called writing one's proverbial memoirs. Nobody but me can get myself out of the hole I'm in, except maybe my dog and that's only because he digs faster than I can. There is also the age old question of: who is the Cosmic Ranger and what does he want from me? You can call him by many names—God; the Great Spirit; the Chairman, perhaps; or even the Karmic Jester (that's what Dylan would call him). But he will follow your ass to the ends of time until you learn your lesson, that much I know. I just haven't found out what the lesson is.

1

*"there's a world where I can go
and tell my secrets to...."*

It is surely significant that the first date I can conjure in my childhood's mind is 1960. That would make me around seven, just about the Age of Reasoning. Even my first LP record, *Around the World with the Chipmunks and David Seville* came out in 1960. Though I was born in the '50s, I was spared any vivid recollection of them—with the exception of Dick Clark and American Bandstand. A telltale staple of my childhood viewing much to my grandmother's dismay, it said a lot about me as a pre-school age child, sitting on the floor in my sleepers rocking back and forth to that primal rhythm. A premonition if you will, of things to come.

I will say that it is obvious to anyone who has ever gotten to know me in the slightest, that music is my frame of reference for everything. I tend to talk in song lyrics and pop music parables. It's a habit I don't remember beginning and there seems to be no end. Music has always been both my salvation and my hell on earth. I have afforded it that much power over me. One of the first things my 6-year-old ears remembers hearing in the ethers, was older school-age children singing "whistle while you work, Nixon is a jerk." I learned that Kennedy, he of the youth and 'vigah' was good, and that Nixon, he of the shifty eyebrows and five o'clock shadow, was bad. Those snippets of early indoctrination weren't lost on me. Perhaps lifelong card-carrying liberals are born into a different kind of awareness. Whereas some sorts of people shut the windows and pull down the shades to a gathering storm, preferring the safe unquestioning mindset of the status quo, some are almost predestined to throw them wide open and invite the tornado in to tea. I was one of those.

My mother has said that I was always rooting for the underdog, always marching for a cause. That's good to know because I was conveniently blessed with being born into an era that had plenty of causes to go around. Like so many of the younger baby boomers, my first clear memory of any historical reference being the Kennedy assassination (I think I missed the Cuban missile crisis), it wasn't difficult to grow up with a healthy distrust of the government and believing everything was a conspiracy. It is no wonder many in my generation are paranoid. Some of us even grew up to create TV shows like *The X-Files*.

For the most part, music that made it to the radio at the end of the '50s consisted of the hit factory out of Philadelphia (conveniently where *Bandstand* originated from), and the Brill Building in New York. Occasionally, a really choice R & B record would rear its fine colored head inside so much white bread fodder, but it was pretty rare before Elvis went into the Army. Those early rock and roll pioneers of color, like Chuck Berry, Fats Domino and Little Richard, still had not been able to break down the barriers of race that divided this country. They may have had hit records, but they still had to enter through the back door. Though something astounding happened at the dawn of the '60s and a guy in Detroit by the name of Berry Gordy, heralded a major cultural shift. He decided to merge two record labels that he had started; one in 1959 called Tamla Records and the other in 1960—Motown Records. It then became merely, Motown, and it was a massive game changer. Not only would it influence American teenagers (including honorary teenager, Dick Clark), to no longer think of music done by black artists as 'race records', but those early Motown recordings, along with those of Phil Spector's girl groups, would travel across the ocean to England, and one day add to the simmering soup that would bring pop culture to a boil.

There was a short period of time between 1961 and '63, where I became aware of the folk music scene. Summer camp counselors had us around the campfire singing Peter, Paul and Mary songs (which I didn't know at the time were folk standards updated or more accurately, watered down to protect the innocent from the more left-leaning sentiments of their authors). And though the name Bob Dylan hadn't yet crept into my daily vocabulary and awareness, he was there nonetheless.

Simultaneously, outside the coffee house scenes of Hollywood and Venice Beach, life in Southern California in the early '60s was everything the Beach Blanket Bingo promotional machine would have you believe. It was a young, money-to-burn, carefree-in-the-sun, hot rod and surf music world. Our rooms had yet to smell of incense and grass but of model car glue, Coppertone and Kool Aid (which, as any red-blooded American kid would know, was best eaten as raw powder out of the packet, turning one's hand into a palette of bright colors). T-shirts were white and logo-less, and we wore ugly plaid Madras shorts with deck shoes. I wasn't old enough to get down to the beach where it was all happening, but with instrumental mood enhancers like "Pipeline" saturating the radio airwaves, the surfing seed was planted in me where it would unexpectedly sprout some 30 years later, taking me back to those summer days of my youth.

When The Beach Boys happened, there was nothing that came even close. The Four Freshman and others of that vocalizing ilk never sang about life in a sunny paradise, where real estate was the primmest in the country, the roads were open wide and dreams were being forged every day by hapless hordes who had all come West to become rich and famous. It was all up for grabs then and despite the blanket of smog that covered L.A. before catalytic converters became the norm, The Beach Boys made the California Dream absolutely gorgeous. Many hours were spent lying on the hardwood floor of my room, my head stationed between the two speakers of my new stereophonic record player that folded up

3

into a carrying case, learning the kind of harmonies that only a tormented genius from Hawthorne, California could have thought up. The Beach Boys, at least in my life, were setting the stage for something totally earth shattering, something so incredible in the History of the World, it can't even be accurately described. The feeling in the air, almost a vibration that, like exceptional dogs, only a chosen few could hear. It permeated every moment of every day leading up to that first night of the *Ed Sullivan Show* on Feb. 9, 1964 when we saw The Beatles for the first time. Like homing pigeons, we all knew where to be that night. That cultural shift was as momentous for us as it was for our elders who had watched a widow following a rider-less horse and a flag-draped casket only three months earlier. For us—it was *that* cataclysmic. We would never be the same.

2

"so you want to be a rock 'n' roll star...."

Little Jewish girls from Beverly Hills with movie star fathers and socialite real estate agent mothers, weren't supposed to grow up to be rock and roll musicians— but that's what happened. It was okay for other Beverly Hills brats to become pop stars, as it was for Dino, Desi and Billy, two collectively the sons of Dean Martin and Desi Arnaz. Or for Gary Lewis (& the Playboys), son of Jerry Lewis. But not for me. Not for this daughter.

My father was Johnny Johnston, a Missouri-born blond dimple-chinned gorgeous crooner who had the distinction of playing a guitar when all the other crooners of the late '40s and early '50s basically stood implanted in front of a microphone. He was nominated for a Tony in 1951 for his role in *A Tree Grows in Brooklyn* on Broadway with Shirley Booth, and was under contract to MGM and Paramount, where he made a dozen or so pictures from 1942 to 1955, like 1947's *This Time For Keeps* with Esther Williams and Jimmy Durante. It was during that picture that he met and started wooing MGM star Kathryn Grayson (*Showboat*), who eventually became his second wife. Kathryn was making *It Happened In Brooklyn* at the time and Dad had enlisted Durante (who somehow was in *both* pictures) to be his messenger boy, carrying love notes back and forth between the two sets. This infuriated one of the heads of the studio, who was in love with

Kathryn and so, just like that, Dad was suddenly let out of his Metro contract.

My mother told me a fascinating but tragic story of how the role of Julie La Verne in *Showboat* was originally given to Lena Horne, but because of 1951's now antiquated Production Code (which wouldn't allow interracial couples to be shown on the screen), the part was given to her friend Ava Gardner. Lena was heartbroken but so was Ava, who really didn't want to take the role away from Lena.

My mother had a wealth of stories such as this and should have written her own book.

My Dad recorded a slew of songs that he popularized such as "Old Black Magic" and "Laura" (which reached Number 5 on the charts in 1945). He *could* have introduced the song "Unchained Melody" *(*from the movie *Unchained,* in which he played a piano playing convict), which was later to become a huge hit in my era by The Righteous Brothers. But Dad decided that since Sinatra didn't sing in *From Here To Eternity*, neither would he sing in *his* picture!

One day I would discover I inherited that propensity toward self-sabotage in my own career. Not only that, I would attract and be attracted to other people that did the exact same thing .

I find it to be yet another irony in my life that my father had the starring role in one of the first quintessential rock and roll movies, *Rock Around The Clock* and that he hated rock and roll and never let me forget it. I have the lobby poster from that movie and my Dad's picture and name are prominently displayed on it. In the 1956 film, he played the pipe-smoking promoter who 'discovers' Bill Haley. He also delivered the very first lines of dialogue in the picture.

My mother Shirley was a gorgeous brunette from Miami, who at barely seventeen, met the producer Joe Pasternak in New York while she was attending the American Academy of Dramatic Arts. He gave her the clichéd "I'm going to make you a star", then held her screen test for him the same day that Eva Gardner had hers. Unfortunately, two days later the Japanese bombed Pearl Harbor and Mom got scared and ran home to Miami. She married a nice Jewish boy at nineteen and had her first child, my brother, Kalman (KC).

After that marriage fell apart, she found herself in some rather interesting company, spending time with a very famous singer who shall be nameless. However, it was not my father, who became her second husband (much to that famous singer's dismay, who had called my mother from the opposite coast, warning "Don't marry the bum!"). She was Dad's wife number three, and Mel Torme' was best man at their wedding. My childhood had as its backdrop, one big movie set. Some of the stars and personalities of old Hollywood that passed through my very tender years as either a family friend or nearly extended family were, of course Mel, Frank Sinatra, Jackie Cooper, Milton Berle, (who had a mad crush on my grandmother, Leah), Mickey Rooney, Ann Miller and Jerry Lewis. And of course, 'Aunt Katie', Kathryn Grayson.

I spent much of my earliest years being shunted around between L.A. where I was born, Miami, where my maternal grandmother lived and New York, where we resided right before my parents separated. I lived like Eloise at the Plaza. My fondest memory of living at the prestigious 55 Central Park West (the gothic building which appeared in 1984's *Ghostbusters* movie), were the doormen all in gold brocade, and the fact that the Macy's Parade balloons would go right by the front windows of the building. Unfortunately, we lived in the back of the building. But that didn't stop me from begging the people down the hall to watch the parade. You could practically touch the balloons as they went by.

My funniest memory living there, was the Christmas that John Drew Barrymore came banging on the door drunk, looking for his wife, actress Cara Williams, who was my mother's best friend. He stumbled in and fell down into our sunken living room, ending up under the Christmas tree.

Some 15 years later, he would be friends with the first man I would ever fall in love with—a famous pop star who, by happenstance, did more than a passing impression of Barrymore's more undesirable attributes..

The Cosmic Ranger tilted his head as if to listen, and smiled a watchful smile.

My parents had separated by the time I was seven, and so we moved from New York back to Los Angeles, and straight to my father's ex-wife Kathryn's house in Santa Monica. It wasn't just a house, it was a Tudor-style mansion that had been built by one of L.A.'s most famous architects, Elmer Grey, who had built the Beverly Hills Hotel in 1912.

In November of 1961, sometime after I had turned 8 years old, Mom and I moved to a cute little house in Franklin Canyon, and just in time for the Bel Air fire. We ended up being evacuated but did not lose our home, unlike the 484 other poor souls who did.

By the time I had that first exposure to the mesmerizing plague from England that had swept over America's youth in 1964, my mother was newly remarried. The conscious decision I made as a child that year became the driving force behind my every thought and action for the next 20 years and even now, tends to color how I view the world. That decision was more than just an act of absolute rebellion, more than just a need to be noticed or understood. Because, though I got plenty noticed, I went and threw out any chance I had of ever being understood, by going against every possible norm of the time for girls my age.

I decided that I wanted to grow up to be just like The Beatles or The Stones or The Byrds or—you get the picture? And in a world where it was okay to put pictures of Paul McCartney up on the wall and dream of one day capturing his affections, you weren't supposed to wonder how he came up with the bass line to "Paperback Writer" or "Rain" (back to back, the two most innovative bass lines of their time in my humble opinion). You weren't supposed to stand in front of the mirror, chin jutted forward with self-assurance and attitude, 'playing' John Lennon. But for this little girl from California, living a lifestyle that was eons away from the dirty docks of Liverpool, it was all that mattered.

The first real tip-off to my mother should have been the ritual cutting off of my long-haired curls and proudly displaying my new Beatle-bob. I wore rings like Ringo on the last two fingers of each hand, and started taking bongos to school. My cheap little Japanese transistor radio was permanently affixed to my ear, and I traded in my Breyer plastic horse collection for an old Spanish nylon string guitar. I then got down to the business of totally alienating every human being I came into contact with, from my predictably horrified mother to every adult authority figure and member of my supposed peer group. All I talked about was the latest record I had acquired, mostly by stealth, rarely by allotted allowance. The other kids didn't quite know how to react. Their fear would often manifest itself in awkward cruelty. I got into a lot of fights. I usually won.

But it was worth it because let me tell you what it felt like then to hold a brand new vinyl 45 record in your grubby little hands. It was better than the biggest bowl of Wil Wright's ice cream, ever. OK—Ben and Jerry's. It was like holding a shiny black circular key to a magical universe, where a secret language was revealed only to you and no one else, especially not your parents. And held them I did, each with utter reverence and a feeling that they were the salve for anything the world could throw at me.

Occasionally though, somebody would come along who understood, if even for a moment. One of those was a girl named Karen Gessler who lived down the road from me. She said her mother knew Brian Jones of The Stones. I was very impressed with that fact and did my damndest to impress Karen, who looked exactly like Cathy McGowen from the British TV show *Ready Steady Go!* I know now that I must have had a crush on her. Every time I saw her at school, it was like a major revelation. She had the longest most perfect straight bangs I'd ever seen, and was the precursor for my fascination with dark-haired, blue-eyed beauties.

Very few pictures exist of me from that time, but an interesting thing occurred in 1995 when *The Beatles Anthology* was being released. On a local TV station in L.A., they showed some footage taken 30 years earlier outside The Beatles' Benedict

Canyon hideaway, just a couple miles away from where I was conveniently living at the time with my mother and step-father. Called 'Edgewood', it was the now legendary location for the infamous Beatles/Byrds summit in August of 1965.

There, in grainy black and white, standing out in the crowd amongst much larger kids, was my 11 year-old self! Representations of my early surf rat phase were in evidence, with my wide-striped Jan and Dean-type T-shirt from Penny's and my St. Christopher medal around my neck. No doubt I had ridden my Hobie skateboard up there in a last attempt to hold onto my distinctly Californian identity, before becoming completely and utterly Anglophiled. But the Beatle haircut gave me away. That and the affected Liverpudlian accent I tossed about as the reporter was talking to us kids, and I could clearly hear my child voice through the din (oh, how embarrassing).

Later, they caught me on camera embarrassing myself some more by running and jumping onto the limousine as it made its way out through the gates. I remember seeing Paul in through the window, just days before I would be screaming my head off at him in mass hysteria at the Hollywood Bowl. How funny. How strange.

I would share a beer with him in a London recording studio overlooking Oxford Street just 8 years later.

3

"stop—hey, what's that sound?...."

The explosion heard throughout the city in the summer of 1965, was written down in the history books as the Watts riots. I was lost in the rather privileged insulated world of the white upper middle-class and viewing the riots from Beverly Hills was truly bizarre. I remember feeling angry and guilty at the same time. The kind of guilt I had always felt as a protected and pampered white kid living in plenty, while I constantly noticed others who had so much less. At my parents' social gatherings, I was often finding refuge in the kitchen with the 'colored' help. Somehow, it just felt more comfortable and real there.

Like a punch in the stomach, I remember exactly where I was when I first heard "Eve of Destruction" in the autumn of 1965. I was at a girl's house who was a George Harrison fan that I had met somewhere and she lived toward the valley side of Coldwater Canyon, which was the next canyon over from me. The dreadful pall that I felt with that record was unreal. I think I stopped breathing. The death knell of the drum, the simple acoustic intro and the sandpaper voice of Barry McGuire combined, sent chills down my spine. And I remember after that, becoming acutely aware of the name P.F. Sloan in association with, not only that song, but other songs that graced my 45s and album covers, which I read voraciously word for word. It is no wonder that I could recite the producer, writer and every group member of any band off any record of that time.

A little more than 20 years later, Phil Sloan and I would become embroiled in a turbulent 9 year yo-yo of a relationship which rivaled that fabled topsy-turvy trip down a well-known rabbit hole.

In March of 1966, there came the rains. With that, a leaky roof and an unexpected stay at the Beverly Wilshire Hotel. Staying at the same hotel, in town for some recording at RCA Studios—were The Rolling Stones. One of the tracks recorded during those sessions was "Paint It Black" and according to Phil Sloan, it was *he* that saw a sitar sitting in a corner of the studio and suggested they use it on the record. I had yet to see The Stones in concert but I got a close up and personal view during that few days. I sought them out amongst the gilded hallways and golden elevators and discovered to my absolute horror, that Bill Wyman and Brian Jones were only a little taller than myself. That summer, Herman's Hermits stayed at the very same house The Beatles had rented at 2850 Benedict Canyon. This time I managed to sneak in. And I don't know how I started this rumor, but indeed, I was Peter Noone's 'cousin' that summer. I ended up knowing Peter over the years and he never let me forget this embarrassing chapter. That's ok. Not long ago, I gave him my entire Herman's Hermits collection for posterity.

I managed to get into a lot of places as a kid and whether I had a story to cover me or not, somehow, whether by magic or sheer savvy, I was present during a lot of freeze frame moments from that glorious place and time. From the time I was just 11 years old, a year earlier, I was sneaking out from the safety of the cocooned canyon and down to the Sunset Strip, where I would wander up and down the street like my older teenage counterparts. I had 'Byrd glasses' in three different colors. I wore a black leather 'Lennon cap', 'whale cords' and De Voss-style shirts, hoping that it would set me apart from the giggling silly little girls in go-go boots and heavy makeup, whose mission was to get one of the guys in a group. I wanted to meet the guys in the groups too, but not for the same reasons.

Like kids who cluster outside a baseball stadium with baseballs in their hands, mine was an act of hero worship. If I could have dragged my pathetic little guitar with me down the hill, I would have. My mission that summer was to find out all the variations on the D chord so that I could play just like Jim (Roger) McGuinn of The Byrds, famous for his Rickenbacker 12-string guitar. It wouldn't be until 1975 when I would finally own a Rickenbacker—a mint condition vintage 1966 Fireglo 360-6, with the checkerboard trim on the back.

The Teenage Fair was an event held during the summer at the Hollywood Palladium, just down the street from the illustrious Wallach's Music City (now gone) at the corner of Sunset and Vine, where listening booths were all the rage and Phil Sloan said as a kid, he had met Elvis. The Fair was a mecca for everything from the one-hit-wonders like The Knickerbockers, whose "Lies" had everyone thinking it might be The Beatles in disguise, to Sonny and Cher and their minions of wannabes in fur vests and bellbottoms.

It was where I had met and hung out with an outrageous, early psychedelic group calling itself The West Coast Pop Art Experimental Band. I ended up being inexplicably trained by some guy to sit in and do their light show (ostensibly, during his 'bathroom break'). That guy, according to Domenic Priore's *Riot on Sunset Strip*, was most likely Buddy Walters, who pretty much pioneered those water and oil light shows. And I was still just 12 years old.

It was the year I met Rodney Bingenheimer, the self-proclaimed 'Mayor of the Sunset Strip', who later was Davy Jones' stand-in on The Monkees TV show and had a major crush on Cher, but would settle for her little sister Georgeanne. Many years later, he would become a well-known DJ on L.A. station KROQ with his show *Rodney on the ROQ*. I met a host of legendary L.A. characters such as Vito Paulekas and his gang (who were the official dancers at Byrds shows), Kim Fowley and Sky Saxon of The Seeds (who picked me up once hitchhiking).

Rodney and his crew would often go over to then KHJ's Channel 9 TV station on Melrose, near the Paramount lot and manage to get into the taping of one of L.A.'s best dance shows, *9th Street West* hosted by KHJ DJ Sam Riddle. Rodney and I used to laugh about the time I was cornered in a room at his house by a well-known musician scenester who exposed himself to me. I defended myself by burning the tip of the guy's prick with a stick of incense and took off running.

My fave hang out on the Strip was the classic '50s-style coffee shop Ben Frank's (now a Mel's Diner), whose close proximity to The Trip nightclub across the street made it the perfect grandstand from which to view the comings and goings of L.A.'s pop elite; Neil Young in his trademark tasseled suede jacket and sideburns; Phil Spector in his 3-piece suit and dangling watch chain, and David Crosby in his iconic green suede cape.

I remember somebody pointing out Terry Melcher to me. He didn't get into the pages of *16 Magazine* or *Tiger Beat*, no, but he had major street cred with me because he had produced The Byrds' first two albums. Terry was Doris Day's son. He had the rather unfortunate distinction of being the man Charlie Manson was seeking that fateful night in 1969, up in that house on Cielo Drive (more on my 6 degrees connection to *that* place later).

Melcher was also a prominent participant in the scene surrounding The Beach Boys and their assorted cronies, having worked with the pre-protest Phil Sloan when he and Steve Barri were doing back-up vocals for Jan and Dean as The Fantastic Baggys. I am still amazed that with all the crossed paths in common, Sloan and I had never once run into each other up on the Strip. But then again, when you're a 12 year old kid, you're literally standing out in the cold with your nose pressed against the glass.

Heading east down Sunset from the Trip was a club called Pandora's Box, a pink and lavender spectacle of a place where on any given day, you could find a dozen runaways stationed inside up against its dayglo walls. Pandora's is cemented into L.A. lore as being ground zero for the infamous November 1966 Sunset Strip riots, immortalized in The Buffalo Springfield's ode "For What It's Worth". What started out as the cops cracking down on 10 P.M. curfew violations, escalated into several days of heated confrontations between them and hundreds of kids just peacefully gathering. In one of those Forrest Gump moments, I missed the acclaimed rocking of the bus that day, but I had been there only a few hours before.

Directly outside the club, on a concrete median at that intersection of Crescent Heights and Sunset, I was for a time, one of the junior activists in Art Kunkin's army, handing out copies of his seminal progressive paper, the *L.A .Free Press*.

The Trip and Pandora's Box (both gone), Ciro's (now the Comedy Club), the Sea Witch (gone) and the Whisky A Go-Go— venues whose memories are still alive in me and to this day, whose ruins or rebuilt facades, I still take visitors to, on my own version of Maps to The Stars.

The Hullabaloo, which had been the '50s landmark club, the Moulin Rouge, was frequented by a local group out of Westchester, who had once been a surf band called The Crossfires. In 1965, they grew their hair, replaced their reverb with jingle-jangle and became The Turtles. It is a bit peculiar that I never saw them either in my traversing of Hollywood.

30 years later though, their drummer Don Murray, would ask me to marry him.

1966 marked the last year any of us in the States would ever see The Beatles in concert again. In L.A., it was at Dodger Stadium and was the second to the last show ever, which of course was held in San Francisco at Candlestick Park (that's gone too). Living in this city most of my life, it is hard to believe that it was the one and only time I had ever been to Dodger Stadium.

There is nothing one can adequately say to describe what it was like to be at an actual Beatle concert. Suffice to say, it was enough to realize the enormity of the fact that you were just breathing the same air at the same time. I was more than fortunate because years later, I learned that it was often who you knew that got you a coveted Beatle ticket. My mother knew a lot of well-connected folks in her real estate circles, so there I was.

That was the year that Mom was already separating from my stepfather, actor Rick Jason (*Combat!*). Rick and I had gotten along famously since he was very encouraging toward my guitar playing. In fact, he was the one who gave me that old Spanish guitar, which by now, I had painted with red and green polka dots (I deserved to be flayed alive for that). He was also the one who had taken me into Westwood Village two years earlier to purchase *Meet The Beatles*, the American version of the black and white British LP, *With The Beatles*. When Mom and Rick split up, I felt I was losing my first mentor and I guess I took it hard, though I didn't realize it at the time.

In October of 2000, Rick Jason died from a self-inflicted gunshot wound. He never even left a note. I had a real hard time trying to explain to his widow, just what he meant to me by getting me my first Beatle album and my first guitar.

My mother and I moved from the Benedict Canyon house to an apartment on La Cienega Blvd. in what is now West Hollywood. As luck would have it, the Fountainview West, (now the Westview Towers) was a block south of the Sunset Strip, which gave me unfettered access to all the places I used to have to sneak out to only the year before. I was now within walking distance of Ben Frank's and the Whisky A Go-Go.

And it was there, in my 12th year, as I stood kitty-cornered to the Whisky, I caught my first glimpse of a tall, dark and handsome 21 year old named Gene Clark, as he entered in through its side door. His tortured presence in my life two decades later, would leave me with haunting questions that have yet to be answered.

Biding his time, the Cosmic Ranger lifted a bridle from off a rusty nail.

That summer, my adolescent reign of terror began. "Psychotic Reaction" by The Count Five came out and I couldn't get it out of my system. It pretty much summed up the whole enchilada.

4

"rebel, rebel—how could they know?"

I started failing in school, big time. Not because I was stupid, but because I really didn't give a shit. I also began questioning the system, as it was becoming painfully obvious back in the relatively dark ages of 1966, that there were separate rules for boys and girls. I didn't dig that one iota and pretty much let everyone know it. And oh yes, it was also the year I discovered both boys—and girls. I had been messing around, exploring sexuality with several little friends and I was as precocious in that arena as I was with my burgeoning peculiar brand of sarcastic humor (gleaned from Lennon in *A Hard Day's Night* no doubt). I got in a lot of trouble.

It was the year I started getting suspended or thrown out of schools with clockwork regularity. Not for anything major, mind you, but silly things like drawing naked pictures of my classmates doing—well, silly things. Or for smoking (or pretending to smoke) *outside* the school grounds. Naturally, I would be the one to get caught every time. And the one that really dates me: for wearing a skirt that went too far above the knee! Remember the ruler, ladies?

I didn't fare much better in summer camp either and had racked up a couple of those by the time I had outgrown them. I can't remember why I was tossed out of one in particular, but the other one was quite a story. I was found in the middle of the night with a little boy camper, hiding in the straw up at the archery range. What were we doing?

Well, we were *both* thrown out and years later, I ran into this little boy. He was a grown man who ran a pawn shop in Hollywood and damn if he wasn't responsible for retrieving my beloved stolen Rickenbacker in the '70s. I didn't even remember his name when I ran into him. But he certainly remembered mine!

By now, drugs had become a way of life amongst the L.A. musos and hangers-on and I saw kids younger than myself who were already screwed up beyond belief. I don't know how it happened that somehow I was spared that, but I can honestly say that I didn't smoke my first joint until like, 1969. As hip as I thought I'd already been those first years of the youth culture, and as surrounded by drugs as I was by the beginning of 1967, I did not give in to peer pressure. I think it was partly due to a desire to be in control. I already took a lot of risks, this hitchhiking little kid up and down the canyons and the Strip. I was daring in a lot of ways. But drugs just didn't appeal to me. I wanted to be completely aware of everything that was going on and to have my wits about me, even as a 13-year-old. It was an amazing time to be alive and I must have suspected that, because I didn't want to miss a damn thing.

The love-in in Griffith Park with The Strawberry Alarm Clock for instance. Hearing "Incense and Peppermints" live had to be one of the highlights of that year for me. That and the release of two life altering albums—The Jefferson Airplane's *Surrealistic Pillow* and The Beatles' *Sgt. Pepper.*

1967, for anyone who was there, whether they were enveloped by a rapturous purple haze or simply unencumbered, comes off in the memory as an intense flurry of colors, sounds, exotic aromas and snatches of cosmic conversations, fleetingly encountered in some really trippy places. Usually you didn't recall how you got there or how you had left. But as history has shown, the artists and music of that celebrated year were so astoundingly brilliant, complex and creative, that it became the watermark for everything that followed. There was this ethereal buzz in the air. Every sense was heightened to almost pre-orgasmic intensity. Young people were opening themselves up to the deepest, darkest depths of their existence by explorations into what had only been known to a few cutting edge writers and artists of previous generations, but was now being entered into by a legion of white middle-class kids. Some survived the orgasm. Some did not.

And if they seemed a little edgy as they handed out flowers to the 'straights' that would come to gawk at them like animals in a cage, underlying all of that was a war both at home and abroad which overshadowed the peaceful vibe. It was impossible to ignore.

I was too young to participate in the growing anti-war movement, but I was aware of the body counts on the TV nightly news. I guess it didn't affect me as much as it should have, as much as it did my older cohorts, for as is the case with young teenagers, they really are into their own trip (in my case, music). They're not really thinking stuff like that affects their world. But ever so subtly, I remember my anger building at the slightest provocation.

So it was that I officially entered into the counterculture. I carried my own freak flag high with my own sense of Us versus Them. The teachers that I would butt heads with daily seemed to single me out and made me the whipping girl for every possible infraction, real or imagined. From 1966 to the ending of the school year in '67, I had been thrown out of three schools. I still don't know what I did.

By this time, Mark Lindsay from Paul Revere and the Raiders had moved into our apartment building, and Monkee Davy Jones had moved down the street. I made it a point to go and borrow sugar at both places. I once ran into Marvin Gaye in the elevator. I found out many years later from Berry Gordy's daughter Hazel, that Motown artists were put up in that building when they were in town. It was after Tammi Terrell died and I said to Marvin in a brave little voice "I'm really sorry about Tammi." From the look on his face, he was very surprised at this little white kid who could not only recognize *him*, but know who Tammi Terrell was! If only he'd known how I had once stood in front of a mirror practicing various Motown dance steps for hours on end.

I would be driving through Lyon, France in April of 1984, when I started to hear his songs simultaneously on several stations. They mentioned his name over and over interspersed amongst the French. That is never a good sign.

1967 was also the year I started painting Twiggy eyelashes on my lower lids, cut my hair like hers and wore dangling Mary Quant colored ball earrings that were interchangeable. I had unwittingly transformed into the Gloria Stavers' *16 Magazine* version of a teenage girl that year. Never quite learned to giggle and act dumb, but I started to become really conscious of fashion, besides what the guys in bands were wearing. I bought Yardley makeup because model Jean Shrimpton wore it and discovered dayglo colored fishnet stockings. This phase wouldn't last very long, but it certainly made my mother happy.

Of the remaining treasures from 1967, I hold most dear— an actual piece of Pete Townsend's guitar, procured from *The Smother Brothers Show* appearance, a segment of which was shown in The Who's film *The Kids Are Alright*. After all the places I have traveled in the world and the many times I have moved, it is hard to believe that piece of Vox headstock with a few strings hanging from well-tarnished machines, is still with me (and no, it is *not* for sale).

The *KRLA Beat* was a little fold-up paper circulated by the radio station of the same name, and it was the bible for teenyboppers like myself to get the lowdown on where The Beatles were in any given week. There were doppelgangers of the same paper corresponding to other stations in other cities, and one day, I saw an ad for a pen pal which had been placed by a Herman's Hermits fan (I was still admitting to that) in San Francisco. Her name was Edie and she and I started corresponding.

But it was Dena, her pen pal from North Carolina who had moved in with her, that became my friend for life. So totally opposite, from radically different backgrounds, for some reason we hit it off, though she still really hates it when I call her a hillbilly.

Dena has seen me through more insane changes and accepted me for who I am without question, more than anyone in my life. Over time, I told her all of my secrets.

All but one.

At the dawning of 1968, in January, with my mother out of town in Palm Springs, I decided to get the hell outta Dodge. I boarded a Greyhound bus and headed for San Francisco. Had I really known what was happening there, I would have gone straight to the Haight. But alas, I ended up at Edie's which was closer to the avenues.

I never got to see the Haight in all its (by then, dying) glory because my mother tracked me down. I was put kicking and screaming onto a plane by poor Dena and sent back to L.A. But my instincts were right on. San Francisco would continue to hold a pivotal place in my life.

Something was shifting in my psyche around that time, and I went inward and embarked on a very strange search for God, through of all things, the Catholic church. I never knew at the time that my father's side of the family were Catholics. I was brought up with basically nothing in the way of religious dogma except that my mother had dabbled in Science of Mind. But we were Jewish, or what I like to call 'deli Jews'. And my Jewish grandmother was none too thrilled at my choice of spiritual training, however brief my dabbling.

When I started studying with the Paulist priests from the church down the road, it must have been an *oi gevalt* for her. I actually received a document saying I had completed the course. I had a rosary that hung from the corner of my bedpost and that was about the extent of it. That little rosary got to earn its keep just a few years later, during the 1971 Sylmar earthquake.

Meanwhile, my mother was worried about my withdrawal and deepening depression, and I was sent off to my father, who at that time was living in Puerto Rico with wife number five. On the side, he was seeing a lady who would eventually become wife number six. I didn't last long in Puerto Rico—all of six weeks. But at least I got to see the rain forest.

Homeboy heroes and UCLA spawn, The Doors, who had made their mark at the Whisky, just happened to have a lot of business happening in my neck o' the woods. Jim Morrison was living at the Alta Cienega Motel just down the street from our building, and Electra Records was further down the road. My mother was friends with their manager at the time and it was cool for me because I would get all their albums marked 'promotional copy'.

I was picked up hitchhiking one day by a red-haired girl in a VW bug. It turned out to be Pamela Morrison. She let me know she was Pamela Morrison, even though I didn't realize the significance of that until after Jim had died.

On the night of June 6th, 1968, my mother came in to wake me up some time after midnight. I thought I was having a bad dream. I know I heard her say "Senator Kennedy's been shot."

The next morning, I hopped on a bus and made my way down to the Good Samaritan Hospital where I stood in vigil outside, along with so many others, tearfully looking up at the window of Bobby's room. In another Forrest Gump moment, it was there that I saw Coretta Scott King at the window, briefly looking out . And as the whole world knows, she had just lost her husband, Martin Luther King Jr. only two months before. I can't imagine the amount of strength it took for her to immediately get on a plane to Los Angeles in order to support Ethel Kennedy, so soon after her own loss. A monumental profile in courage.

1968 was the year that officially put the nail in the coffin of America's innocence. To have lived through it was to have felt the collective air being knocked out of the entire country and reverberating throughout the world. Everything after that heated up pretty damn fast within the socio-political activist community. It culminated in one big bloody head-bashing bang at the Democratic convention in Chicago and gave rise to a new kind of television reporting, a kind of voyeur journalism if you will.

Nothing after that night where "the whole world is watching", could be hidden from the cameras again.

5

"time it was, and what a
time it was, it was..."

I had been relinquished to a small tumbleweed-ridden Mormon enclave posing as a summer camp in Utah for the summer of 1969, when I heard the news of the passing of Brian Jones. He was the first of my generation's rock icons to fall and it was impossible to conceive of. Nothing was more profoundly sad for driving home the alienation I felt amongst these junior proselytizers, who would hound me at my bed bunk at night with their admonitions not to drink that daily cup of British tea I took pleasure in. Certainly The Rolling Stones were the epitome of the Devil's work on earth, so for the remainder of my stay there, I became the representation to them of all that was evil. I couldn't wait for September.

And then, late that October, I became aware of Sandy Tarbet for the first time, as we huddled around a bunch of dirty wooden lunch benches at Fairfax High School. It started out simply with a line of dialogue from *A Hard Day's Night*. I threw one out at her, complete with full Beatle intonations—and she answered me right back in kind, straight from the script.

She had passed the test.

Little did I know that she would embark me on a journey that would lead both of us to everything we had only dreamt of, since that fateful night in 1964 when, like ravenous sponges, we collectively absorbed the Beatle oracle into our childhood psyches.

Sandy was the first of my soul mates on this earth. Of course, I was immediately smitten by that dark-haired, blue-eyed, porcelain-skinned look I found so captivating. Her story began growing up as a real 'red diaper baby'. Her father had given janitorial jobs to some of Hollywood's blacklisted elite, and there were books in her house to be quickly hidden if an unexpected knocking on the door would materialize. We would find ourselves in mid- conversation on the phone when, if there was any static or clicks on the line, Sandy would nonchalantly say, "Hello, J. Edgar." My only previous frame of reference to that kind of stuff had been *The Man From U.N.C.L.E.*

She knew early on she had found the perfect songwriting partner in me even before I did. I knew I had found the perfect chisel for my rough-edged rebelliousness, the perfect glue for my scattered intellect, and the buffer zone between my perceived misunderstood self and the whole big bad world. Sandy held it all together for me and kept me focused for the next 14 years. Through her I would learn the meaning of dedicated partnership and of devotion to a nearly impossible dream against all odds. Through her, I would truly understand the beautifully exhilarating and sometimes painful process of creating a work of art, whether it be music or the written word.

But most of all, I would learn about selfless, unconditional love and how rare a gem that is. Sandy always validated me, while recognizing my weakness underneath my hard exterior and making it a strength. How she did that, I do not know. A Pisces taming of the Scorpio dynamic perhaps.

But even so, to this day, she is the only one who can call me on my shit.

I turned sixteen right after we met and I was anything but sweet. Being even then an incurable romantic, I'd often pass myself off as a cross between a total hippie, a jaded rock and roll scenester, and a Renaissance lady-in-waiting. And it was around that time that I got to put all those personas into play, the night I met Leonard Whiting.

Leonard, who was heartthrob-du-jour in all the teen mags, due to his magnificent performance in Franco Zephirelli's *Romeo and Juliet*, was being shown off at a Beverly Hills party by his agent at the time, one, Rudy Altabelli. Rudy was the man who happened to own a house up on Cielo Drive in Benedict Canyon, that he had rented out only a few months previously to actress Sharon Tate. The rest was gruesome history.

My mother was going to Rudy's party that night and decided for some reason to take me along. It was there I met Leonard and he asked me to come up and see him the next day at the house he happened to be staying at. You know the house—the one that made headlines when 'pig' was scrawled in blood upon its door?

Leonard seemed to be a bit intrigued with me which was an amazing compliment, he being the absolutely gorgeous creature that he was. We agreed to keep in touch and did over the years. I would often visit him in London and we remained friends even later through his marriage, when I would babysit his daughter Sarah. By then, of course, I was on a different path with Sandy, but in the early '80s after Sandy and I had parted and Leonard was divorced, he and I hooked up whenever I was in London. He had a great sense of humor, was a wonderful talent and a gentleman, and should have worked a lot more than he did. I would encounter a lot of key people like that through my life. Unique and talented artists who, after a tremendously promising breakthrough, had their progress arrested midstream. I, myself, would become part of that unfortunate syndrome.

Romeo and Juliet: tragic ill-fated lovers. A symbolic motif I was woefully destined to re-visit.

6

"lookin' for fun and feelin' groovy"

In the summer of 1970, I succumbed to a bribe. My mother had said that if I got anything over a 'C' on my report card, I could go to London for the summer. I pulled it off and found myself at 16 years old, living a dream come true in a tiny bachelorette flat overlooking Hyde Park. I was chaperoned, if you will, by some friends of my brother's, who lived very close by in Lancaster Gate. I proceeded to make their life hell.

One of my better antics that summer was going to a free concert in Hyde Park and bringing back to the flat what my guardians believed to be a "filthy long-haired hippie type." To me, he was lovely. We became fast friends. I learned he was from Birmingham, which in this pop fan's mental file had been the stomping grounds of The Moody Blues and The Spencer Davis Group, so definitely well worth a visit.

We exchanged numbers and the next thing I knew, I was up in Birmingham for a weekend, where one night I found myself in some youth club with The Who performing just arm's length away from me! I had already seen them in the States but never quite like that in their element. Kind of—The Who in their wild natural state. *Tommy* had only recently come out and it was absolutely awesome to hear them doing some of those songs live.

Pete Townshend would turn out to be more of an influence on my rhythm playing than just about anyone and just a few years later, I would be gallivanting around L.A. with Keith Moon and entourage.

Other people I met that summer or hung out with under various circumstances; John Walker of The Walker Brothers, pretty much unknown in the States but once massive in Britain; David 'Screaming Lord' Sutch, who I later saw around L.A. in his flamboyant Union Jack Rolls Royce, and all the members of a Manchester band then called Hotlegs ("Neanderthal Man"), who then became the more well-known 10cc ("I'm Not In Love"). They had just acquired a brilliant recording studio in Stockport in Cheshire, and I had gone to visit a member of the band, songwriter Graham Gouldman, who was the British P.F. Sloan.

Graham had written countless hit songs, for The Yardbirds ("For Your Love", "Heart Full of Soul"); Herman's Hermits ("Listen People", "No Milk Today"), and The Hollies ("Look Through Any Window", "Bus Stop"). I had met Graham at the Beverly Hilton Hotel a few years earlier when he was traveling with Herman's Hermits in the States.

I left London that summer making a mental note for future reference, of where all the best Indian take-outs were. I knew one day for certain, I would return. Back home in L.A., Sandy and I didn't immediately get down to brass tacks and plan our conspiracy to take over the pop music world. It took a bit of major hinting and cajoling on her part because according to her, I seemed to be oblivious as to what was developing. There was in fact, a kind of epiphany when the reality hit us that The Beatles really were indeed, breaking up. And as we mourned what had amounted to our childhood's end, we gathered a sense of purpose somewhat in all that hopelessness.

Finally, it kind of fell into place one day as we were sitting around Sandy's mother's kitchen table, making a list of prospective names for our little merry band that consisted of only just the two of us. By then, we had written some songs (Sandy now professionally, Sandy St. James) and had a vague notion that the world might be ready for a couple of girls who, at first, looked and sounded like a Merseybeat version of The Indigo Girls (though they wouldn't exist for at least another 15 years).

We came up with the name 'The Skiffles'. First, because it ended in the proverbial good luck charm of 'les'. Second, because it was a cute nod to the origins of our heroes, who began as a 'skiffle' band. Skiffle was what Americans would have called 'jug band music', a simple kind of homemade folk music using an array of accompanying instruments that weren't really instruments at all until they had been rigged up, like washtubs (bass) and washboards (percussion).

Newly outfitted in our matching white Oxfords with black laces, armed with our tried and true Beatle-tested weapons of choice (Sandy with her '66 Hofner bass, me with my '65 sunburst Epiphone Casino), we set off to fight the good fight.

It was 1971. A bass playing girl from Detroit named Suzi Quatro, was just moving to England, where she would be taken under wing by record producer Mickie Most, who wanted to fill the void left by Janis Joplin's demise. We were unaware of Quatro clear across the country, but something was definitely stirring in the ethers. As far as we knew at the time, there *were* no females playing electric guitars, forming bands and writing their own songs that got any notice.

With one exception—a Richard Perry produced band that had come out a year earlier: 'Fanny'. Four very excellent musicians, their keyboard player Nicky Barclay having played in Joe Cocker's band, Fanny suffered from the same indignation as us. They were 20 years ahead of their time. The world was not ready for a group of women without makeup, dressed in jeans and T-shirts, who did a lot more than stand there singing without an instrument or playing a tambourine demurely in the background. Fanny rocked and sadly, nobody but a chosen few would acknowledge it.

Giving credit where it is due, I later discovered that the first real female rock and roller came along in the early 1930s, in the guise of gospel singer and musician Sister Rosetta Tharpe. Rosetta could rip like nobody's business on a Gibson SG or any other guitar situated in her very capable hands. I have no doubt that Chuck Berry heard her in his formative years and by the mid '50s, became the one associated with that sound. I also used to think it was Willie Mae 'Big Mama' Thornton (who recorded "Hound Dog" in 1952, way before Elvis) or La Vern Baker (1954's "Tweedly Dee") as the first women of rock, but Rosetta Tharpe laid the groundwork.

Then of course, there was the pioneer session musician Carol Kaye, who, as a member of L.A.'s 'Wrecking Crew' in the 1960s, gave us some of the most distinct and famous bass lines of all time. Her credits take up an entire book by themselves. However, for us in the early '70s, we still felt that we were absolute anomalies. We found that, not only were there no other visible women rock musicians to join our crusade, but the male musicians we ran across were usually totally intimidated.

Though there was one very amazing and memorable exchange between us and Spencer Davis, who was living up above the Strip at the time and to his credit, accepted us completely. He invited us up to his place, where we actually jammed with him on his classic "Keep On Runnin'". A most glorious moment and a reminder that, when one is 18 years old, one tends to be obliviously arrogant and quite fearless.

For the most part though, everywhere we turned, we were reminded that we were rare travelers on this uncharted road for women rock and rollers. We should have learned a lesson from Fanny but alas, we fancied ourselves as having a bigger agenda. That agenda was put to the test the day we met Don Boyd.

Walking down Sunset Blvd. on a sweltering day, was a very pale man in a velvet suit. I knew that immediately gave him away as an Englishman, approaching him bearing the statement, "You must be English." "How did you know?," he giggled through bottlecap lenses. I learned that he was a struggling film producer, proceeded to tell him of my struggling music endeavors and the next thing I knew, I had him listening to our demos. One of the songs specifically targeted a very famous record producer who we had aspirations of impressing one day with our adept and clever songwriting. When Don Boyd heard "George the Magic Man", he said he believed he had just the ticket into George Martin's office.

It really was too good to be true.

7

---

*"how does it feel to be one of
the beautiful people?"*

Sandy and I made our ceremonious arrival in London in the late summer of 1972, and made our way by train up to Liverpool to symbolically await the final word. Within a year, the original Cavern Club, that mecca where The Beatles had made their mark, would be closed and demolished, to make way for an extension of the Mersey rail line. I made it down those stone steps just in time to catch the graffiti in the original women's loo, proclaiming: "John Lennon has the biggest prick in Liverpool."

At the end of September, a once-shining son of Liverpool, Rory Storm, whose band The Hurricanes gave rise to one, Ringo Starr, was found dead with his head in an oven, an apparent suicide pact that had also included his own mother. Well, that was the original story we heard while we were actually there *in* Liverpool. It has since been cleaned up on Wikipedia. Who knows what the actual truth is?

On November 15, 1972, The Skiffles signed a recording contract with Beatles' producer George Martin. Apparently, Mr. Martin hadn't lost his touch for recognizing a creative entity that was not only unique, but years ahead of its time. True, we were a bit derivative (a bit?) of those four Liverpudlian lads who had proceeded us on the other side of Sir George's control room window. But we were women doing this and besides Fanny and a few other lone pioneers, there really was no precedent. I think he saw the potential in the songwriting team that Sandy and I were becoming by then. And the youth factor wasn't overlooked either.

We were only eighteen and nineteen at the time.

But Fate sometimes has a way of thumbing its nose at dreamers whose karma dictates that they get only so close and no closer to the Dream. And it couldn't be a more bizarre irony than Paul McCartney being the one that became the fly for our ointment. Unbeknownst to him, he was the make or break factor in this tale. For just as we felt poised to take on the world, having recorded our very first single, "Teacher Can't Get Me" b/w "I Think Of You", which was to be released on The Beatles' first label, Parlaphone, Paul decided to break the ice with Mr. Martin after a long sabbatical and return to the fold to record "Live And Let Die" for the new James Bond film.

The Skiffles didn't stand a bloody chance in hell.

Though our record did get reviewed in a couple of the British pop tabloids at the time (getting compared to Creedence Clearwater which was a hoot), and did get airplay a few times on Radio Luxembourg (a mainstay of popular and underground music), we never got to pursue the momentum that was built up around us, from the photo sessions and press releases done by the esteemed EMI, to the follow-up single that we were ready to lay down at a moment's notice.

Sandy and I did get to meet all of The Hollies one day over at EMI, but most of what transpired during that time seems like a blur with one exception—the surreal sharing of that bottle of beer with McCartney, as I sat and watched him mixing his first Martin-produced record in several years. He was very kind and encouraging and was especially impressed with Sandy's Hofner bass, as one of his had just been stolen only days before out of a van in Nottinghill Gate. He offered to buy it off her. Bless her heart, she said no.

Everything instantly went from hot to cold, from a fiery proclamation to a dull thud, as we crashed back down to earth. Sandy and I felt like two pricked balloons flying backwards around an empty room. The last straw for me was probably the rather callous remark George Martin had made when we lamented we had run out of money and had nowhere left to stay.

"I know of a few park benches," he said sarcastically.

You know the old adage, you should never meet your heroes, you'll just be disappointed?

I was crushed. So much so that I decided to walk away from it all.

My last act of embittered defiance before we left London, was to throw a milk bottle up at Martin's office window. Our drummer Bill (who wasn't on the session but had flown in from California for moral support) burnt a cigarette hole for good measure, into one of the sofas in the waiting room of the studio complex at AIR London. *So* pre-punk.

Broke, defeated and emotionally drained, we returned to the States to lick our wounds and regroup. But how does one recover after getting so close to the light and then burning to a crisp?

Where do you go after having had the biggest record producer in the world?

Nowhere really. Within a year we were back in England floundering around like lost puppy dogs. By then, Suzi Quatro's second single "Can the Can" was working its way up the charts and we decided to return to Liverpool.

Following breadcrumbs, we further immersed ourselves in the power of myth, perhaps to discover in that place an answer, a beacon to point the way.

We may as well have gone to Glastonbury looking for Merlin, for the only prophecies we discovered were the many profanities spewing forth from drunken Liverpool poets or washed up musicians left behind in the scourge that was Beatlemania. But like any true spiritual seekers, we cast off our cloaks of comfort, lived in the kind of poverty we couldn't ever before fathom, and suffered through the coldest winter two California kids could ever imagine.

It was time to let go of the Dream—just to survive.

The plane ride back again to the States was devastating. Going back to our parents was out of the question. Our vastly different lifestyles and continued pursuit of what remained of our music career would have made it impossible to live with. So we ended up in a crappy one room apartment on Gordon Avenue in the pit of Hollywood, just south of the recording studio at 6000 Sunset Blvd., that had been the site of some of the most famous records ever made.

Groups like The Beach Boys and The Mamas and Papas had gone through those doors at Western Recorders. It was hallowed ground. I will make note here that two very seminal records of the mid-'60s were recorded in that studio, the sheer irony of which you will discover later: "Eve of Destruction" (Barry McGuire) and "It Ain't Me Babe" (The Turtles). We were also spitting distance from Columbia Records studios, where The Byrds had recorded their first two albums.

Every time I passed those studios by, I would cringe at the reminder of what had become of us. The now painful memory of where we had gotten to and how fast we had lost it. For the next two years, we struggled with just the sheer day to day living from hand to mouth. And even though we had several projects going on (one being the 'soundtrack' for a proposed movie idea based on a book), we never recovered the momentum we had lost.

It was 1975. The telltale phenomenon of 'morphic resonance' continued to manifest, for not far away, somewhere in Hollywood, an actual girl group called The Runaways was forming under the tutelage of local producer and resident sicko, Kim Fowley. We had previously had a run in with Fowley when he suggested that Sandy and I would do well by putting on some makeup and maybe showing a bit of cleavage or some such rubbish. I told him I would rather piss on his desk (or something along those lines). Whatever it was Fowley was offering at the time, we didn't want it. And judging by what later happened to certain members of

The Runaways under Fowley's watch, it would appear we made the right call.

Music had become frighteningly bad, what with disco starting to make its appearance and there wasn't much of anything I was passionate about, with the exception of one album by the band I had met 5 years earlier: 10cc. Their brilliantly innovative *Sheet Music* had become mandatory listening for anyone entering over our threshold at the time. Eric Stewart's engineering tour de force still makes my socks roll up and down and it is to this day, one of my Desert Island Discs. That and 1967's *Odessey and Oracle* by The Zombies, which I had only just discovered that year, eight years after its release.

It was the year that we inadvertently found ourselves engaged in yet another controversy, this time quite public.

On a pleasant sunny day down at the beach, on the border between Venice and Marina Del Rey, Sandy and I decided that the beach looked sparsely populated enough to allow ourselves the luxury of being ourselves. When a great shadow was cast over my topless sunbathing body, I looked up to find a big burly cop telling us we had to put our tops on. I guess I was at the end of my rope, feeling like an outcast, so I was determined to stand my ground. After all, I said, this was unconstitutional! I advised the officers to observe some of the men on the beach, their overweight torsos having caused them to have protruding 'breasts' certainly as large as Sandy's little nubs.

It didn't wash. We were arrested and taken to jail. With help from the ACLU, we would become mavericks in an ensuing case that eventually was thrown out because we had no criminal records and we got tired of fighting. But being interviewed on the local ABC news was interesting. For good measure, I decided to do it topless from the roof of our apartment building! The whole debate was a first and as far as I know, the law really hasn't been tested since in the state of California. Well, not legally.

Also, not far away from the roach-infested piece of shit we were calling home at the time, was RCA Studios, where The Stones had recorded their anthem "(I Can't Get No) Satisfaction" in 1966.

It was also where the first recorded version of "Eight Miles High" went down that same year (later The Byrds had to re-record it at their parent company's studio at Columbia).

I can't remember how it was I ended up there one night, but there I was. And it was that night that I met singer-songwriter Harry Nilsson, one of several '60s casualties that I would try to save from themselves.

8

"and now it's only fair that I should let you know...."

Harry was the first truly brilliant person I had ever met. He actually was proud of the fact that he had been for a time, a member of Mensa, that rather elite society of rather boring people that had an inordinate amount of brains. Harry had burst onto the pop scene sometime in 1968 when The Beatles had proclaimed him to be their favorite American songwriter. That alone was enough to put him on the map. He had the ability to be hilariously quirky, poetically old-fashioned, and heartbreakingly insightful, all in one song. His voice was crushingly beautiful. The first time I ever was affected by music so deeply it made me cry, was when I first heard Harry Nilsson's voice.

I immediately found in him an intellectual sparring partner, a challenge. I could throw years of accumulated pop and other trivia out at him and he would leave me in the dust. I liked that. Harry was a statistics man. He could pick out off the top of his head, shit you couldn't believe but you just *knew* was true. He was funny as all get out, but behind all that was a deep sadness that caused in him a self-destructive nature that never left him, until he died in 1994 at the age of fifty-two.

Even that far back in 1975, he was alternating between lines of cocaine and drinking Tequila straight out of the bottle. It was the first time I'd ever seen a Tequila worm. I also found myself wincing every time he would light up a cigarette, thinking about that gorgeous voice.

Harry would nightly have an assortment of very entertaining, also brilliant and talented people around him that kept him interested enough to continually hold court. He almost always was the center of attention, unless of course John Lennon was present. I never got to run into my hero Lennon, but he and Harry made headlines around that time with their antics at the Troubadour one night. Something to do with a Kotex placed strategically upon one of their heads (p.s. it wasn't Harry).

Someone I do remember amongst the funny clowns in Harry's traveling circus, was Douglas Dillard, that beanpole of a banjo-pickin' boy from Missouri, who could nearly drink even Harry under the table. Another case of 6 degrees. At that time, Doug had started to run around town again with an old cohort of his, another tall Missouri-born boy he used to have a pioneering bluegrass band with in the late 60's, called Dillard and Clark—as in Gene.

It would still be more than 10 years till I would fall under Gene Clark's spell.

One of the more fascinating people in Harry's court was Van Dyke Parks. Van Dyke was most well known for having faced the demons of Brian Wilson several years before, having co-written with Brian, the complex and astounding "Heroes and Villains", amongst other masterpieces during the much heralded *Smile* project..

Van Dyke was basically Mark Twain in Hollywood, a brilliant young Southern gentleman who found himself in the cynical netherworld of L.A. rock and roll. Van Dyke didn't escape unscathed either. He had his moments waking up in strange places (amongst them my place; no, it wasn't like that!), but seemed so good-natured and philosophical about it all. Van Dyke was an old soul. He was always amusing and never phony or sordid—pop's answer to Oscar Levant (whose daughter Amanda was once married to my brother KC by the way, and gave him two sons, David and Charlie). However, my friendship with Harry began to have its sordid moments—like the night in the studio where he and I ended up in a compromising position on the floor, under a piano. That was only the beginning. I started to bring him home with me after his sessions and with Sandy there, it just wasn't on. She would do just about anything to suffer me gladly, but this got old real fast.

What the hell was I thinking? It was the beginning of the end for us.

Sandy and I broke apart shortly after that. Harry went back to Una, the sweet Irish girlfriend he would eventually marry and have six kids with, and I embarked on an entirely new and totally unforeseen path.

In the span of a year and a half, I would move to Venice Beach for the first time, get pregnant by a pretty blond Swedish boy, and have an abortion. Traumatized, I moved back to my parent's house and inexplicably went to study acting with Lee Strasberg, leaving my musician persona completely behind. It was too painful a specter to deal with.

I also left behind the person I was with Sandy, who didn't know what hit her when I left so unexpectedly. I thought there was something else I had to experience and proceeded to make up for lost time, by quick and meaningless relationships with several men, one after the other. It was a portent of things to come at a later time in my life as well. I was very unhappy but didn't know what else to do with myself.

I was going out on a lot of auditions, mostly for plays. Out of habit, I continued to hang out in rock and roll circles even though my music career was pretty much shelved. My musician mind however, never seemed to stay very long on that shelf, and so I was still being invited to parties and places where various scenes were happening.

Speaking of shelves, I was at a party at (Three Dog Night) Danny Hutton's place in Laurel Canyon, and I remember I spent the entire night just looking at his book shelves. He actually did have books. I would often do that at gatherings where I didn't really know anybody. You can learn a lot about people from their bookshelves.

I hung out with British pop jazz singer Georgie Fame ("Bonnie and Clyde"), when he came to town for a stint at the Whisky. He was put up at the Continental Hyatt House (fondly known as the Riot House and now totally remodeled and called the Andaz, don't ask me why). I ended up going with him and his entourage to a soccer match at the L.A. Coliseum! I believe it was Manchester United and Milan, but don't quote me.

Oddly enough, around the same time, I was at an actor's seminar somewhere in the valley, and drove actor and fellow l'enfant terrible, Michael J. Pollard home, because he didn't have a car. He had been in *Bonnie and Clyde*, the movie. He was a really groovy cat and just wanted to show me his tattoos.

And a one-night stand I admit to with Beach Boy Bruce Johnston, only happened because we were talking about how we weren't really related after all, as he was adopted! We met one night over at RCA studios, and I can't recall if I took him back to his pad in Brentwood or whether I followed him back. But he did play me "I Write The Songs" (and "Disney Girls" for good measure) on his piano the next morning during coffee!

6 degrees double-whammy: Bruce had been the other half of surf pop duo, Bruce and Terry (as in Melcher), and their big hit was "Summer Means Fun", written by P.F. Sloan, who many years later—see what I mean?

And what else do all of the above circles of people have in common? Every one of them made their initial mark in the '60s. I swear, these guys must have seen the flashing neon sign on my flower child forehead. They were drawn to me like moths to a porch light.

In 1976, Paul McCartney decided to hit the road with his 'Wings Over America' tour. It was very strange to see Paul in this atmosphere again when thinking back on the last time I saw him. But even stranger still, was Sandy and I finding each other amongst thousands of people at the L.A. Forum! We had gone separately, and if that wasn't an indication that the cosmos was trying to tell us something, I don't know what. We reunited after that night and set up house again in a little place near Los Angeles City College. We adopted a part Dingo puppy named Gypsy, and went back to our old life as if that year and a half hiatus had never happened.

9

"if you're going to San Francisco...."

It was 1977, the first United Nations International Year of the Woman. Sandy and I were at a conference celebration and it was there that we met an animated little sprite of a creature named Annie Toone. A keyboardist and one of the only kickass female blues harp players I'd ever heard, Annie kept in touch with us from her base in San Francisco, where she was hatching a plan that seemed to be right along the same line as ours. It was seriously time to pull up stakes and start a new life, and with the growing socio-political gay scene happening there in the Bay area, it seemed like the right place at the right time.

We settled into a one room apartment on Jones Street, in what, for my mother's benefit, I called lower Nob Hill but which was in reality, the Upper Tenderloin. With Annie now swelling our ranks to three, it was time to find a new name for the 'band'.

We decided on 'The Next'—as in, 'Next Big Thing'? We actually got to play the famed North Beach punk palace Mabuhay Gardens. That and a couple of outdoor festivals was about the extent of our gigs. We concentrated on recording some new demos.

The next few years were a flurry of creative activity. Not just songs but two television scripts for, of all things, *Starsky and Hutch*, and a screenplay, *The Power Merchants*. Sandy and I were also involved in the support of Supervisor Harvey Milk's campaigns, most notably the issue of equality for gays, which was in its adolescence as a movement. We participated in a night patrol in the Castro district, after a rash of gay-bashing had broken out.

And we were there that fateful day in 1979, when Harvey and Mayor George Moscone were assassinated by a disgruntled, homophobic ex-policeman-turned-supervisor, Dan White.

My car was nearly subsequently trashed in the burning of automobiles in close proximity to City Hall during the riots that ensued, after a jury found Dan White guilty, not of murder, but of 'involuntary manslaughter'. It was later dubbed the 'Twinkie defense' because White had been imbibing too much junk food in his self-loathing.

Dan White later committed suicide upon being freed from jail.

That year also saw the death of an old acquaintance of mine, someone who I had hung out with during that year and a half apart from Sandy—The Who's drummer Keith Moon. In the mid '70s, my mother had rented he and his girlfriend Annette a house in Benedict Canyon. And as the paradoxes went in my life, he was found dead in Harry Nilsson's London flat.

Keith was (and still is in my opinion), the best rock drummer that ever was (except for Ginger Baker and a guy named Dusty Watson; Google him). His all-over-the kit style influenced every rock drummer that came after, bar none. He was a powerhouse. Most of all, to those who knew him, he was a gentleman. But the downright epitome of the tragic clown.

'Moonie' was one of the most hilariously funny people I've ever met. It wasn't so much what he said, but how he said it. His comedic timing was impeccable. I would tag along with he and his entourage up to Denny's on Sunset (also now gone) for some late night eats, and just sit silently, watching him play off of people and situations. I really believe they based the Dudley Moore character in *Arthur* on Keith. He was the model of the elegantly British happy drunk.

Unfortunately, it killed him.

Music had started getting good again, what with the New Wave scene happening and some would say, the burgeoning punk scene which I found to be more of a catalyst for other forms of expression I wanted to see re-emerging, like performance art and poetry. Actually I wrote a good deal of poetry whilst in San Francisco, most of it created as I huddled under a stained-glass lamp at Vesuvio's, directly across from the famous City Lights Bookstore, where Lawrence Ferlinghetti and the Beat poets were kings.

When our scripts were unexpectedly picked up for representation by a literary agent back in L.A., we were rather stunned. So after 3 years in San Francisco, it was time to return home to face a whole other chapter of rejection and humiliation. We actually got pretty far with both *Starsky and Hutch* scripts—all the way to their story editor, who expressed a great deal of interest.

He was about to get back to us on the matter when the show was canceled! There it was again—just so close and no closer.

We had moved into a little house on Sanborn Drive in Silverlake and Tom Waits' father, Frank, lived next door. Gypsy enjoyed her new backyard, after having been cooped up in a tiny room in the city for so long. We acquired another dog, Sasha, whose part Husky lineage gave her the perfect excuse to try out her escape artist routine. We had an extra bedroom in the house so we took on a roommate, Pamela Scott-Fraizer, who I'm still friends with to this day. Pami was an actress who had also studied with Lee Strasberg and who was doing well in voice-overs and TV.

We never did sell any of our scripts. Being novices going from songwriting to scriptwriting, it was to be expected. But it was good to know that at least we garnered the attention of an agent.

And that *Starsky and Hutch* story editor that saw promise in our scripts? Anthony Yerkovich. He went on to write for *Hill Street Blues* and created *Miami Vice*.

By the middle of 1980, I was ensconced once again at Lee Strasberg Theatre Institute, which had moved from Hollywood Blvd. to a huge white complex on Santa Monica Blvd. near Fairfax. I also returned to the Equity waiver theatre scene, appearing in several plays and receiving good notices as well.

On the evening of December 8, 1980 around 8 PM, I was driving on my way to a club called the Starwood (now gone), which just so happened to be down the road from the Institute. The nightmarish news broke on the radio—John Lennon had been shot in New York.

I nearly veered off the road but managed to pull into the driveway of the Starwood. In a daze, I deliberately walked up to the ticket window and said blankly to the girl behind the glass, "John Lennon's just been shot." Then, as if on automatic pilot, I got back in my car and parked it near the school, where I wandered in looking for anyone who could keep me from falling helplessly to my knees. I found a friend of ours in class and motioned for her to come out. Together we stood there, stunned and breathless, as the world stopped turning.

I don't remember much after that, not how I got home, nothing. The next three days were a blank. I don't remember eating or sleeping. There was the constant murmur of the television, showing the still frames over and over again, of a chubby-faced young man standing in anticipation next to his hero, and waiting for him to autograph an album. It was another one of those beginnings of the end.

10

"this is the end—my only friend, the end"

There wasn't a day that went by since I was 10 years old, that when I picked up my guitar, I didn't see John Lennon's face in my head. He was the beginning for me, the reason I started—and he was the end. I found it impossible to play after his murder, the trauma was that heavy. We had lost so many of our rock and roll icons by then, from the trinity of Hendrix, Joplin and Morrison, to the ultimate godhead himself: Elvis.

But nothing was like this. Not for me. It would send me spinning off uncontrollably into an empty void, un-tethered for years without a foundation or direction. Words like 'goal' and 'dream' were no longer in my vocabulary. I was never the same after that.

I took down my shingle and shuttered the windows. Put my guitar away in its case. I was done.

Since expressing myself through music became a dead issue so to speak, I threw myself into acting. I wanted to be anybody but me. There, I could express all the anger and devastation I felt at my world falling apart. In addition to still studying at the Institute, I got an observership at the Actors Studio West, not quite as prestigious as the one in New York, but still attracting that rare breed that only the Studio could. It was during this time that I honed the sense memory and emotional recall exercises that would one day help me access memories in my own life that I had buried.

I got heavy into James Dean, adopting a serious tortured expression and wore a leather jacket and horn-rim glasses to all the late night underground clubs that were popping up all around Hollywood in the early '80s. I actually started hanging out with one of Dean's old friends, Maila Nurmi, who was more well known in the '50s as 'Vampira', the precursor to Elvira, Mistress of the Dark. I would play bongos behind several local poets, when not sitting in a corner brooding. I had no qualms about nearly shaving my head for the stage production of *Playing For Time*, about the women's orchestra at Auschwitz. It fit in well with the minimalist existence I seemed to be seeking.

Drew Barrymore, younger sister of my first childhood friend, John Blythe Barrymore, made her stage debut in that play. Right after that, the world would know her as the precocious and adorable Gertie in 1982's *E.T., the Extra-Terrestrial*.

Sandy didn't like the change in me at all. I would stay out till three or four in the morning. I was drinking a lot—beer mostly, but just two beers for me was a big deal. If there would have been any time I would've gotten into drugs, it would've been then. As it was, I only dabbled; a snort here (hated it), a toke there (much better). I preferred to suffer through this period relatively coherent. I was once again blessed by that good ol' built-in self-preservation mechanism.

I got my Screen Actors Guild card in the midst of all this, appearing in a picture I've never seen in which I played, what else, a tormented juvenile delinquent. The grooviest part was getting to do my own stunt when I got 'hit' by a car. Ran out in front of it, leapt up over the hood, rolled onto my back and grimaced in pain. They cut to place blood coming out of my mouth. It was awesome. Can you say, no budget?

Sometime later I got to appear on the TV series *Quincy* playing a punk; shorn hair, spike bracelet and all. Played a female cabby in Francis Ford Coppola's *One From The Heart*. Was in the nuthouse scene in *Frances* with Jessica Lange. I was naked in that one. Yes, but so was Angelica Huston.

But one of the most profoundly disturbing things I ever worked on, was a TV movie about what it would really look like—if the button were pushed. I hear tell the entire country was riveted to their screens the night *The Day After* aired and apparently, it so alarmed Reagan that he upped the ante by developing his Star Wars missile defense system.

Then I broke into voice-overs. Seemingly out of nowhere, I got a call from the actor who had portrayed Sherlock Holmes in the play of the same name, in which I played his young boy assistant, Billy (I was *that* androgynous). He needed someone who could convincingly do the voice of a 12-year-old boy. Thus, I worked steadily in voice-overs for years after that and was happy to find a working gig that I actually dug.

I was still hitting the after-hours clubs (often hanging out with actor Laurence Fishburne), and occasionally going out to shows on my own, since Sandy really wasn't all that interested.

One of the shows I remember going to in 1982, was at a club called the Palomino in the valley. I went to see former Byrd Gene Clark perform live for the first time. While nothing too momentous happened that night (we didn't meet)—4 years later I'd be at that same venue, watching him from the shadows in a totally different scenario.

The Cosmic Ranger saddled up. The cattle were movin'. The lassos were ready.

By 1983, life with Sandy and life with any cohesiveness or meaning kind of went out the window. I don't know why I left, except to say that maybe I was nearing my Saturn return (that craziness that often happens as one approaches thirty). I was going through some major changes and everything I had known and been familiar with had to be sacrificed in the process. Much like Lennon did when he buried The Beatles and went off with Yoko. That was *his* Saturn return.

It would be more than a decade before I would experience the feeling of 'home' again. I also had told myself early on, that

I would never just play music to amuse myself as a hobby. It was all or nothing. It was the Scorpio way. I chose at that point in my life: nothing.

For Sandy, the sense of betrayal and loss was enough to send her back to her mother's house, where she stayed for years and didn't find another relationship until well after the millennium. We were both a mess. Not counting that time apart in the mid-seventies, Sandy and I had been together for 14 years. Neither one of us had even turned thirty yet.

That year, my grandmother passed away and left me some money, and even my parents agreed that a trip to Europe might not be a bad thing. I don't think that living in a Volkswagen bus for a year and a half, was what they had in mind. Our dog Gypsy, who had gone through all the changes in locale and lifestyles along with us, was left with me, and I was at a loss what to do with her while I was away. Luckily, I found someone to take care of her. I thought I was only going to be away 6 months.

When I arrived in England this time, I literally became another person. I changed my name to Chova Lee (taken from the Gypsy word, *chovanni,* for 'witch'), and almost as in days of yore, took my knowledge of herbalism on the road, becoming a traveling healer. I did many of the neo-pagan and hippie-type festivals, sequestering myself within the much maligned community of the 'travelers'. I partook of the sacred mushroom for the first time. I found myself living out the ultimate hippie dream, doing everything I couldn't do in the late '60s because I was too young and could only be an observer.

But I had taken notes.

I had never been to 'the continent', not in all the trips to England I had made. I decided to look up somebody that I had met briefly, back during my recording sessions in London— Denny Laine of Wings.

Denny was the former lead singer of the first edition Moody Blues, whose vocal on their first hit record, "Go Now", will hold up a hundred years from now. Denny was then on the lam from the tax man, living in a predominantly English enclave on the Costa del Sol in Spain. I don't even know how I found him, but I did.

It was where I spent my 30th birthday, surrounded by virtual strangers and drinking red Spanish table wine out of a bota bag.

A little black and white dog, that looked remarkably like Nipper the RCA Victor dog, had adopted me, and I named him Sam. He lived with me in my VW bus and kept me company. Even though I rarely played, I kept an Epiphone 12-string acoustic with me. I picked it up one day and played for the first time in a long time, while I was in an English style pub. I must have been slightly drunk (me?—drunk?). I remember I did a rather embittered rendition of "Working Class Hero".

Finally after 3 months, I had had enough siesta and decided to make my way back to England, but not before taking a ferry from Genoa, Italy to Greece, where I traveled up through Macedonia and what was then peaceful Yugoslavia. I went through places that would one day be obliterated by war. Going back through Italy, I did the whole tourist trip in Venice, Florence, Milan and Rome. Back in London, I began hanging out in a coffeehouse grotto in Earl's Court called the Troubadour (not to be confused with the renowned venue of the same name in West Hollywood). It was there that I joined the Troubadour poets and started giving poetry readings. I found a group of eccentric people there that most certainly appreciated my twisted sense of humor, which was a rather difficult commodity to convey in the States. I had rather a grand time and am still in touch with some of those folks on Facebook.

I was at a little informal parlor gathering at a flat in Bayswater, where a friend of mine I called 'The Alchemist' lived. Terry rarely showed his mystical prowess in the various and sundry arts, but I was drawn to him and the people around him. So was Denny Laine's ex-wife Jo Jo (though for different reasons), who I had become very close with.

One night at Terry's, I happened to notice a tall, attractive, long-haired gentleman from across the room. I wasn't wearing my glasses and it wasn't until I got up and walked past him, that I noticed him watching me.

Then I realized it was Jimmy Page.

I remembered back when Sandy and I were trying against all hope to find a melodic, simple lead guitar player, and it seemed that everybody was hell bent on playing like Page, being the rock god, just heinously riffing away. It kind of left a bitter taste in my mouth so, with the exception of say, "Stairway To Heaven", "Kashmir" and a few other songs, I was not a big fan of Led Zeppelin. I kind of had a mental block about them.

However, it was Jimmy's earlier band from the '60s, The Yardbirds, whose every record, I had bought. And I could name every member of the group which, for a time, also included guitar icons Eric Clapton and Jeff Beck! You would think in the course of conversation, I would get around to mentioning The Yardbirds (or even Zeppelin). Nope. Not even once.

Jimmy and I started talking mostly about the magical arts. Though I knew his musical history, I knew very little about him personally. I did know that he was into collecting stuff on Aleister Crowley, though I don't know how I knew that. I think I broke the ice with him when he told me he was about to go into a studio again with Robert Plant (which would have been The Honeydrippers project), and I joked, "Oh, you're not going back to *that* racket again, are you?" He cracked up. I doubt if anyone had talked to him like that in a long time.

Later that night, one thing led to another, specifically outside to my van. I would have several encounters with Jimmy over at our friend Terry's flat, which seemed to have become a magnet for both of us during that time. Nothing out of the ordinary went on, you know, just the usual boy/girl stuff, pretty innocuous.

However, it would seem I had dodged a major bullet of some sort, for years later, I learned from a friend, some of the more scandalous stories about Page that had been written in books about Led Zeppelin. Stories involving whips, handcuffs, you name it. I'm like, "Oh my god—what?!" But to be fair, Jimmy has said in interviews that these accounts were basically all salacious rubbish—and, being that he was ever so sweet to me, I would rather believe *him*.

Back on the road, I camped for days at Appleby Fair (the Gypsy horse fair held in Cumbria in the north of England), where full-blooded Romanies were actually coming to *me* for both advice and medical attention. It must have been my chosen surname of 'Lee', one of the most common Gypsy names in Britain. A lot of them were even redheads!

And the experience that changed the way I looked at everything, the Summer Solstice at Stonehenge, where I got to stay for the very last Free Festival, before they put a fence around the stones. Before the cops starting coming in to hippie bash. It became known as the Battle of the Beanfield, where 537 people were arrested, trying to get to the stones. Hawkwind would play every year and that year, 1984, was no exception.

It was a powerful experience and very important for me as a woman to watch my nurturing side developing. It seemed I may have been the sole herbalist in the entire camp, and people would come to me for help, whether it was for a bad trip or a sprained ankle. I could feel a distinct softening process, the Earth Mother taking over the part of me that once was so hard and cynical, in order to protect myself and to be competitive in a (rock and roll) man's world.

The path of most resistance, became the least. It really was like having a big boulder drop from off my shoulders. And to think I would no longer have to keep pushing it uphill—or so I thought.

I returned to the States to find that Gypsy was still where I left her and waiting for me to come home (I would *never* leave my dogs now). Though I had no idea where home was. Even after the revelations about myself in Europe, I was a stranger in my own hometown, having no idea who I was or where I belonged.

So Gypsy and I ended up staying in Glendale with a lady I had met at a pagan gathering, a High Priestess who taught classes in Wicca. I figured it would basically be a continuation of what I was delving into in England. For a while, I threw myself into 'women's spirituality', participating in the Wheel of Life rituals that make up the religion. That happened to be quite compatible with a gig at the Renaissance Faire, where I worked as just your basic bodice-clad wench at the 'gypsy camp'.

I found myself to be coasting along somewhat autonomously, without too much noticeable loneliness or sense of isolation—until one day, I picked up my guitar and started writing songs again. Possibly motivated by listening to some of the more political songs in the women's music scene, I began returning to some of the social commentary Sandy and I used to do so well. It was also time to start going back out into the music scene, to see what it might possibly have to say to me, if anything could be salvaged. Turns out, I was about to once again get down to the business of salvaging yet another '60s lost soul—or two.

"hey, Mr. Tambourine Man, play a song for me"

On January 11th of 1986, I found myself back on the Sunset Strip, at a place called the Central (now the Viper Room, where River Phoenix met his fate).

There he was again, the man I had last seen in 1982, when I was a vastly different person. I was just paces away from the very place I had first laid eyes on him, 20 years previously in 1966, as he was entering through the side door at the Whisky A Go-Go. But now I was no longer a child. I was a full-blown endowed redhead, who was often going braless in gauzy little hippie blouses, adorned with colorful necklaces and Gypsy shawls. A "Stevie Nicks in a Madonna world" as a friend so aptly put it many years later.

That must have caught his eye because, after the show, despite being surrounded by people and in the middle of several different conversations at once, he looked directly at me, leaned over and whispered, "May I have your number?"

I knew he was dangerous just by the look in those piercing blue eyes.

Gene Clark, the tall and handsome dark-haired Byrd, the one center stage playing the tambourine, singing in a plaintive melancholy timbre that gave you goose bumps.

He had been the main songwriter of the band, and his songs on the first two Byrds albums were the ones I zeroed in on as a kid, the ones I always found most compelling and mysterious. Of course, The Byrds had become famous for covering Dylan and putting him on the mainstream map, but knowing that someone in the group had actually written songs like "Set You Free This Time" and "Here Without You" was stunning, even to me as a pre-teen pop connoisseur.

Gene had been only 20 years old at the time.

When he left The Byrds in the spring of 1966 (having just delivered his classic "Eight Miles High" for good measure), I remember consciously never buying another one of their records. Oh, ok, I bought "Mr. Spaceman". But I absolutely refused to accept the Gram Parsons (or any other) line-up. Parsons was no Gene Clark, that much I knew. Though I will cut him some slack since he wrote a song that later would become kind of an in-joke between me and Gene, a song called "Hot Burrito #1".

In later years, I still bowed in deference to McGuinn and the holy church of Rickenbacker and bought a couple of his solo albums. And yes, I had bought some of Gene's. But where The Byrds were concerned, that's holy grail stuff and I'm just a purist, I guess.

Apparently, so was David Crosby. According to John Einarson's excellent book *Mr. Tambourine Man - The Life and Legacy of the Byrds' Gene Clark*, Crosby said, "The Byrds were done when Gene left; we were never the same after that. I always said there were only ever five Byrds." Chris Hillman concurred: "The five guys, that's The Byrds, the original five."

Gene would find out throughout the rest of his life just how true that was. He could never escape what, in one sense, became his own Sisyphean burden.

If Harry Nilsson had been the first voice to bring tears to my eyes, Gene's just left me shattered and totally mystified. I had started listening again to his 1974 masterpiece, *No Other* for some odd reason, and that was what prompted me to go to the show that night. I didn't even intend to say anything to him, but just stood there gazing at him, marveling at how ruggedly handsome he still was; that often photographed chiseled face with the high Indian cheekbones, those intense blue eyes. He was still built (as my friend, writer Domenic Priore had observed), "like Paul Bunyon", with those broad shoulders and strong arms.

And the thought crossed my mind for a few split seconds, as my eyes drank him in: "Oh my god, if I give him my number and he actually calls me—what then?" The attraction was immediate and intensely sexual.

The Cosmic Ranger struck a match and threw it onto an already burning pyre.

I didn't have any paper so Gene got a pen from somebody, and he rather stealthily wrote my number on the inside of his wrist. And then, as he got swallowed up by the crowd around him, I slowly crept away, turning back to look at him one more time. If I had been a cartoon, there would have been a bubble above my head saying, "What just happened?" I honestly didn't expect to ever hear from him.

Having been out of the L.A. music scene for quite some time, I basically knew nothing of the trail of drunken and drug-addled destruction Gene Clark had left in his wake throughout this town. Sure, he looked a little rough around the edges now and he wasn't that 20-year-old I remembered from The Byrds, nor did he have to be. But I had all kinds of experience, hanging out with crazy, drunk musicians and laughing at their antics as I sat by completely sober. I was always good at being one of the lads, wasn't I?

I was soon to find out that Gene was looking for a lot more than that.

When he finally called just a couple days later, all my savvy and sophistication, all my cool L.A. blasé just went right out the window. I was physically shaking. His animal magnetism, coupled with a self-effacing country boy charm, just seemed to reach right through the phone and send sexual twinges through my body. Something in that soft-spoken, yet whisky-soaked voice told me, I was in for one helluva ride. Not that he wasn't sweet and gentlemanly. He was definitely all that and more.

Gene was brought up in a small semi-rural area outside of Kansas City, Missouri and came from a family of 13 kids. It wasn't exactly Ma and Pa Kettle, but to someone like me, he may as well have been Huck Finn. His story after he left Bonner Springs, Kansas in the fall of 1963 has been well documented. How his first big break came from being discovered by Randy Sparks, who brought Gene into The New Christy Minstrels; (6 degrees: my brother Denny first joined The Christys in 1967, and still continues to work with them off and on today). Gene then made his way to L.A.'s Troubadour, where he met young Jim McGuinn and David Crosby.

The rest was Folk Rock history.

Unbeknownst to me, the Gene Clark that I was about to rendezvous with in my 1973 mustard yellow VW bus, had gone through years of severe alcohol and drug abuse, one failed marriage that produced two sons, and a trash heap of record labels that wanted nothing more to do with him. I had no idea about his violence, his unpredictable mood swings, and his penchant for surrounding himself with drugged-out leeches and opportunists, who took advantage of his weaknesses and enabled his self-destruction. Astonishingly, throughout his anguishing travails, after he had had a major nervous breakdown and left one of the most successful bands of all time at the height of their success in 1966, he had produced an incredible body of work almost from the get go. He never stopped writing heart-wrenchingly beautiful songs and had recorded at least ten post-Byrds albums by the time I met him.

'Geno', as his friends called him, had a solid Mid-Western work ethic that managed to stay intact throughout the worst of his misfortunes. That and his vulnerable, raw talent was what made so many people try to consistently help him and give him just one more chance, even as it seemed to all fall apart before their eyes. They knew when he was sober, what a sweet and gentle soul he could be.

But then they encountered his darkness.

Consequently, Gene had burnt a lot of bridges in this town. But he was about to be given a new chance and a new project to keep him focused.

In the summer of 1984, Gene had been introduced to Carla Olson of The Textones, a cow punk band that had been playing around town and had graced many an ad in the LA Weekly. I was not unaware of her, being that she was a woman in a band and had been friends with The Go Go's Kathy Valentine, who she had originally formed The Textones with. The fact that Carla also played a Rickenbacker back then did not go unnoticed by me either. At the time, she was being managed and wooed by a friend of friends of mine from Fairfax High, Saul Davis, who took on the Herculean task of becoming Gene's manager.

Meanwhile, I should have noticed the way Gene stealthily wrote my number down as being the ominous sign that it was. I found out that, no, he wasn't exactly married, but he had been seeing this woman on and off who was one of those enablers I mentioned earlier. She had been a drug dealer for years and had already participated and spectated in Gene's downward spiral for a decade; to the point where, I was now trying to hold together the shell of a broken man who was on his way to an early death.

Besides the alcoholism (though he was supposed to be on the wagon at the time), I didn't know why he was sometimes in pain. Not just his bouts of mental anguish, but actual physical pain. It would be 25 years before I would learn exactly what that pain was, so adept was he at hiding his malady from me. I knew that sometimes, in the heat of passion, we had to slow down and take it easy as something was obviously hurting him. I thought it could have been a result of his drinking. I was naïve, I didn't know. But one day, I would.

Eventually, I was more than pleasantly surprised to find out that it's true what they say about a guy who can play a mean harmonica.

When Gene wasn't gigging out of town on his never-ending 20th Anniversary Byrds tribute tour (which I found terribly humiliating and so did he really, though he never complained publicly), or recording with Carla Olson on the amazing album that would become *So Rebellious A Lover,* we would mostly rendezvous at a restaurant/bar just walking distance from his house. It was called the Lamplighter (now called Corky's, as it had been in the '50s), and there we would huddle in the semi-darkened corner booth, like a couple of truant teenagers.

I was not a drinker and I've always hated American-style bars (as opposed to quaint British pubs), but I wasn't actually allowed to show up at his house unannounced, because of his living arrangement (which at one point got even more complicated when his two sons came to stay). That had me on pins and needles, for Gene had to be the one to call me. I couldn't call *him*.

A friend told me decades later that this scenario seemed to be right out of The Stones' song "Backstreet Girl". I didn't realize in the beginning that Gene was being secretive, not so much because he was hiding *us*, but because he was hiding his hiding place, and that he was being protective of me, keeping me away from what he called 'the cesspool' his life had become.

He called me his 'good girl'. I didn't smoke, do drugs or drink more than a beer. My usual beverage of choice had been then, and still is, a simple cranberry juice with a slice of lime. Knowing what I know now, that nearly every woman he had been serious with up till then, had been tainted by some kind of major substance abuse, I can see why he protected me.

Thus, time spent with Gene was incredibly intensified, because we never knew when we could be together. There was a night, sitting in our little booth at 'the Lamp', the memory of which can still leave me tossing and turning at night in pleasurable agony.

I was sitting close to Gene, so that his right hand was under the table up under my long skirt. I had no underwear on and I realize I must have done that on purpose. Buoyed up by liquid courage, and right there in the crowded bar, he was nonchalantly doing something to me under the table where nobody could see. Periodically, he'd look into my eyes with this powerfully feral smile. Finally he knew he had to get me out of there quick, so he took me outside to my curtained van, and right there in the parking lot, he finished me off.

It was the single most erotic thing I've ever encountered in my life.

Gene could sometimes turn even a mundane act of sexuality into a heightened mystical experience. Thus, he would become the standard by which all other men would be judged.

He was an infinite study in dichotomy, seemingly shy and self-conscious one moment, but then turning as sultry as any Jim Morrison pose. And when he was drunk, he could morph into the worst shit-kicker hick that ever graced a red state truck stop. His usually soft-spoken and gentle demeanor could suddenly shift into fearful paranoiac visions, as if he was dangling over Dante's inferno. He could be deeply empathetic and totally absorb another's pain, and then just as easily, explode into a whirlwind of anger, triggered by some unseen force, striking out at anyone and everything.

I know now that much of Gene's paranoia and sometimes an uncharacteristic bravado, was fueled by a little white powder that I seemed to be in total denial about at the time. Perhaps that was how he was able to ask me for my number that first night.

We were out at the old Trancas Bar and Grill in Malibu one night, and a guy may have looked at me more than once I guess. Gene went ballistic. He shoved the poor guy up against a wall and it was about to get worse, when I somehow got him out of there, just as the management had called the cops. We had to run across the street to the beach and literally lay low in the sand dunes until the coast was clear. Gene was oblivious to the danger, laughing and using the occasion to make out on the beach, from where we could actually see the threatening lights of the police cruisers!

As time went on, I learned to accept the many fractured elements of his personality, mostly because he needed someone to love him for all that he was, even if made malevolent by various substances. Sometimes it was like being inside an emotional memory exercise at the Actors Studio. Within the confines and safety of the secluded stage we created, he so needed to just be himself, however that manifested.

Sometimes it was breathtakingly beautiful. Other times, it was downright frightening.

Me and my VW bus became Gene's rolling shelter from the storm—a storm he reluctantly had to navigate through in public, having to follow his own breadcrumbs. I knew he just needed a safe place to be quiet and to rest. The boy was tired. His small rented house in Sherman Oaks was often party central, a circus, with people coming in and out all the time.

Then there was the constant psychodrama with that other woman in his life that I perceived as being the complete opposite of everything Gene needed to be healthy and centered. Besides Saul and Carla, I may have well been one of the few people around him then, that was completely sober. And like Harry Nilsson, Gene smoked like a chimney—an absolute crime with that beautiful voice.

Whether it was in the van or at my vintage Hollywood apartment at the renowned Villa Carlotta, I offered Gene a safe haven, a place to be where he could quiet the demons in his head for a while. Sometimes, we wouldn't talk at all, but just watch the sunset over the ocean or listen to each other breathing. Often, he would bring a notebook to write, and at those times I would just be grateful to allow him that quiet sacred space. Other times, we could talk for hours; then I would lie next to him and watch him as he slept.

The intensified moods Gene was prone to, due to what I now surmise could have been aggravated by cocaine, would keep him in a state of exhaustion. His whole being was crying out for rest and inner peace. How he knew the night we met that I could offer him this without either of us uttering a word to each other, I'll never know. We would 'talk story'. He deflected away from himself a lot at first and wanted to hear about me. Naturally, he was blown away at my George Martin tale and decided he could top it, by telling me he nearly beat the shit out of a certain music mogul, who disputes that to this day. But Gene sure enjoyed telling the story, whether it was embellished or not. We went through that "Oh yeah? Well, listen to this one!" like a couple of kids and it felt so good to have someone to do that with, someone who understood at least some of where I had been. It lessened my disillusionment and I think it helped him deal with his as well.

I never brought up The Byrds, unless he did.

The real turning point for us on trust, came on a night when we were parked on Mulholland near Beverly Glen, just over the hill from where he was living. We were also very close to the Benedict Canyon house where, back in 1965, Gene had gone with the other Byrds to where The Beatles were holding court, and he was king of the world then. How fragmented he must have felt recounting that legendary story (which of course, I already knew but I let him tell it anyway). How outside of his own space and time he must have felt. Because as we both started to cry over the loss of John Lennon, Gene's sobs started to wrack his entire body.

It was then I knew, that he was crying for losses that went way beyond the murder of our hero. Though he had been drinking earlier, still, I was stunned. I'd always loved a man who was free to cry, but Gene breaking down like that took my breath away, and I didn't know what to do. So I thought of something that had happened a couple years before when I was in Spain.

There was a young guy who had been viciously attacked by a dog, so a bunch of us threw him in the back of a car to take him to the hospital. It was obvious he was going into shock because he was crying and shivering. He just wouldn't calm down. So to distract him, I did something so unexpected, yet so natural. I pulled up my top and gave him my breast. Instantly, like hitting some primal chord, the young man's face softened, and he went into a deep calm. His shaking and crying stopped.

I did the exact same thing for Gene—and lo and behold.

After that night of exposed vulnerability, over time, he'd slowly open up to me, like a rushing river held captive in a bottle. We talked about so many things, though the exception seemed to be about his family back home. For some reason, that made him uncomfortable. There was a lot of pain there. It seemed there was nobody who he felt he could trust, who hadn't used that exposed heart against him. Suffice to say, I have kept his secrets for decades and I will, still.

Though, I would find out years later, Gene didn't tell me everything.

There are some things he told me that I have wanted his two sons, Kelly and Kai, to know—like how happy their father said he was when he first fled L.A. in 1970, taking refuge up on the Mendocino coast. Gene had found complete fulfillment there in life with his new young family. He wrote some of the most astounding music of his entire career, immersed in those surroundings.

When Gene would speak of Mendocino, his face became radiant and his voice, almost reverent. Then would come the sad silence that told me a thousand tales. Indeed, there was a part of him that was yearning to go back to that simple way of life, before the pressures of the music business, coupled with alcohol and drugs, left he and his family life in ruins. Perhaps I represented that possibility to him—this unabashed hippie girl who had lived with Gypsies.

After I told him those stories, he went, "Wow, you're the *real* Gypsy Rider!" I didn't know what he meant by that, until much later when he played me that devastatingly gorgeous song of the same name, which eventually ended up on the *So Rebellious A Lover* album. Later he would play me his studio work tapes and I was enthralled. It would one day turn out to be his biggest selling album.

It was also the last studio album he would ever make.

I started to keep my Epiphone acoustic in the van, in case he got inspired. He would play mostly, because I felt my chops weren't all that good by that time. We never played a Byrds song, though I did do Dylan's "The Lonesome Death of Hattie Carroll", a song which I barely remember today.

Gene had a haunting cowboy whistle on him, the likes of which I had only heard in old cowboy movies, and from one other—my own father, who also came from Missouri.

We would hide away in our secret lover's cove in Malibu, or park up at our hilltop sanctuary, high above the coast highway just outside L.A. county line, where the night sky and the ocean became one giant velvet painting. Our first sojourn up there, Gene made sure I would remember it for the rest of my life.

And as I lay on my back being absolutely ravaged, I looked out the rear window, and through the van's parted curtains, I could see a billion bright stars shining through my ecstatic tears.

In the morning and many other mornings thereafter, we would speak of heading north, never to return. Over time, that Mendocino dream would become our escape plan, and I would have followed him in a heartbeat if he had seriously acted upon that promise.

We got as far as Ojai once. We stayed there for nearly 3 whole days. Gene even showed me off to some artist friends of his who lived up there (obviously they were not part of the L.A. crowd). I didn't see him take a drink the entire time.

We laid on a hill, in a field full of wildflowers, and we watched the clouds go by, naming each cloud by its shape. As his body covered mine, shading me from the sun, I hardly noticed when I got stung on my thigh by a bee. The next day, we window-shopped in the town. All of it, glorious moments of 'normal', where I caught a glimpse of what life might be like with Gene, away from the poison that was L.A.

I watched how he and my dog Gypsy would play together on the beach. Gypsy adored Gene, and I often thought that if he had had a dog to anchor him, it would have made all the difference in his state of mind, at those times when his world grew darkest.

We spoke of karmic love, lovers who recognize each other over many lives. He would one day write a song about these mystical conversations, though I wouldn't hear it for decades. We felt like we were trying to catch up on lost time, to remember who we might have been in said other lives, so deep was the need to crawl up inside each other, to hold on tight through the night.

I didn't realize it then, but Gene was desperately grasping the last vestiges of his own life force, as it was slowly slipping away.

One of the most beautiful things he said to me, was that he wished he had met me after his wife left him in the mid '70s, that "things could have been so different." I remembered when Doug Dillard was working on the Nilsson sessions back in 1975. It would have been so easy for Doug to have brought Gene down there to RCA, while I was there at the same time. But it never happened. I wasn't ready then.

The harsh reality was, at least in this life and at that moment in time, it was too late for Gene. It was too late for us. He couldn't just look off into the sunset, look back at me and say with absolute certainty, "Let's go." I knew he had obligations here, perhaps a new chance at success (but fearing that it would bring him to his knees again, as it had in the past). He had tried to live both lifestyles at the same time, but the sordid pull of L.A. had always won out.

Eventually, the place with all its dangling, deadly treasures, would destroy him.

12

"they've given you a number, but taken away your name"

With the exception of being at some of his local gigs (where I kept a very low profile), I was seeing less of Gene into 1987. He was either working (good) or unable to get away (bad), though he would often call from some hotel or pay phone and leave funny cryptic messages, addressing me as 'James'. Sometimes it would break my heart into a million pieces, just to hear his voice. I physically ached for him.

"Hey darlin'—you're beautiful, you know that?"

Was it to keep me hooked? I hated my cynical thinking, but I was becoming bitter with the situation of always literally being at Gene's beck and call, although I had encouraged it.

I told him to keep my number in his wallet in case he was in trouble. What that meant was, getting a call at 3:30 in the morning, with Gene on a pay phone, standing drunk somewhere on a street near Sunset Blvd. but he doesn't know exactly where. At that point, I was pretty much willing to suffer through anything with him in order just to be with him. I allowed him the freedom of showing up at any hour of the day or night in any condition, and I never once turned him away. And though he said he was protecting me from his other world and the seemingly bacchanalian goings on over at his house, it felt awful still being what amounted to his dirty little secret.

Though to be fair, at that point, I already had my *own* dirty little secret.

One night, I got a real good look at what my future might have held with Gene, when I was finally over at his house with a group of people. He had gotten into a fight out on the street with the girlfriend, who temporarily was on the outs and staying away. They used to break up every other week. He had warned me, "I don't want you hurt; I'm no good for you", and something about dragging me down into the cesspool with him.

That night, I saw my first real example of how dangerous Gene could be, when the *other* girlfriend showed up at the door. He chased her away and then I heard him threaten to kill her. He came in frantically looking for a gun and it took two guys to hold him back! That's when I had to get out of there. His face was terrifying.

Later, he told me he was just angry and did that 'aw shucks' Missouri boy on me, "I didn't really mean all that stuff." Then what *did* he mean, and what would have happened if he *had* gotten to his gun? I dredged up Lennon's murder and told him in so many words, I don't do guns, ever. It was not part of my lexicon.

There was that part of Gene that was still the good ol' boy, into motorcycles and things, those things being guns and knives. It scared me to death.

Gene was just too unpredictable—which of course, made him all the more exciting.

I remembered my old friend Malcolm Evans and what his fascination for guns did to him. Mal was a big lovable bear of a man, who had been the loyal and ever-present road manager and chief bottle washer for The Beatles, from day one. No one saw more of the Beatle phenomenon on a day-to-day basis than Mal.

But when it all came to a crashing halt, so did his life. He didn't know what to do with himself; got divorced from his wife, losing his family and stability. He then moved to L.A. (big mistake). He took up with a nice redheaded lady named Fran, whose little daughter Jody, I just happened to baby sit for.

In January of 1976, Mal had taken some valium and was really out of it in the upstairs bedroom of their house. Fran was freaked and called the police. They say he only had an air rifle, as he sat on the floor beside the bed, facing the bedroom door. That's when the LAPD barreled in and plugged him full of holes. He died instantly.

So no, I don't do guns.

For some reason, not long before I met Gene, I started hanging out with an old scenester I used to see when I was a kid up on the Strip. I would see him everywhere and never knew his name, which turned out to be Hal Marshall. Having gotten to know me and maybe having even read some of my lyrics, he called me up out of the blue one night and told me he wanted me to meet someone who was playing that night in Hollywood, somebody he said would blow my mind. In fact he said it would be "a meeting of minds." The man was probably never so astute in his life. Perhaps he was sent by the Cosmic Ranger to throw me one surefire wicked curve ball, because things were about to get even more complicated.

March 2nd, 1986—the night I met Philip (P.F.) Sloan.

He was making a rare appearance at a club called Raji's on Hollywood Blvd. The first thing I did was to saunter up to him, arrogantly place some of my lyrics down in front of him (a protest dirge called "Blades of Hypocrisy"), and said "read this"; there was that old teenage arrogance again.

He did so, then looked up at me with the biggest brown Romanian eyes I'd ever seen, and said, "That's the best thing I've read in years." I still don't know what possessed me to do any of that, especially the calculated touch of having worn what could only be construed as a vintage P.F. Sloan-type corduroy cap, to mess with the guy's mind. I left the club that night without even so much as a good-bye.

A week later, Sloan had tracked me down and gotten my phone number from Hal (who mysteriously, I never saw nor heard from again). He invited me over to where he was living and *had* been living, for too long a time alone. I didn't know then that he had always been alone (even in a crowded room), but I knew when I entered the place, there was something off kilter.

I found him fascinating, in that wounded animal sort of way. You could see it in his eyes, hear it in his words. Tragedy permeated everything around him. Another broken down '60s songwriter.

Thus, he was irresistible.

So bit by bit, I learned of *his* heartbreaking story. A middle-class Jewish kid transplanted from Queens, N.Y., who was rock and roll crazy, got his first guitar as a child and got very good, very quickly. He made his first record at thirteen. Went from record company to record company, carrying his guitar in a pillow case. Eventually was signed as a songwriter for $25 a week and started cranking out songs, some of which actually got placed.

Until one day, a guy named Round Robin had a minor hit with a song called "Kick That Little Foot Sally Ann" (which I actually remember hearing as a little kid), and Phil Sloan had arrived.

By then, working for producer Lou Adler and his nascent Dunhill Records, Phil and his songwriting partner, Steve Barri, became The Fantastic Baggys to record back-up vocals for Jan and Dean. The Baggys even recorded their own album, today a coveted collector's item. Phil had his hand in quite a few of the early '60s vocal surf records.

Thus it was with much trepidation, that people took him seriously after that, when he became instantly world renown in the autumn of 1965. A song he had written at the age of nineteen, hit number one on the charts.

The song was "Eve of Destruction", and it would hang over Phil like an epitaph. He became a virtual hit-making machine after that: ("Secret Agent Man" for Johnny Rivers, "Let Me Be" and "You Baby" for The Turtles and "Where Were You When I Needed You" for The Grass Roots). But the political fallout after "Eve" was so intense that, after a game of psychological warfare with the powers that be, he was virtually shown the door at Dunhill (threatened with being thrown out of a window, he told me).

At barely 21 years old, there was nothing left for him to do, but implode. What followed was a 20 year exile, in which Sloan would stare into a shattered mirror of madness and self-loathing. The man I was sitting with, in a dark and dingy apartment in 1986, the man whose name I remembered through a 12-year-old's eyes, was the forgotten hero whose words had actually changed the voting age in this country. He was the lone survivor of a nameless war, alive when by all accounts, he shouldn't have been.

I later wrote a song about Phil's tale of woe as the indentured songwriter held captive, called "The Jester of Dunstable Hill".

It wouldn't be long before Phil Sloan became *my* dirty little secret. I know I probably wouldn't have pursued anything further, if it hadn't been for Gene still seeing that other chick—a case of instant karma, I guess. I wasn't being vindictive, just truly inexperienced in the ways of men. I never learned all the rules (read: games) that young girls do by the time they're in middle school. So I winged it.

Besides, I was to discover that Phil had a legion of ex-girlfriends and alternates hanging around. So all that served to do was to make me more brazen with my tall, dark and handsome hidden lover on the other side of the hill.

With Phil, there was none of the pulsating sexual chemistry that I had with Gene. It was mostly cerebral. I knew Phil was attracted to me, but I was to learn he was a bit dysfunctional in that area, perhaps just another layer of his damaged persona. He always had a bad case of the darting eyes and sweaty palms. As time went on, I gave him every opportunity to express himself fully, but he was never really comfortable in his own skin and I didn't know why. In all the years I knew him, there were only a couple of times where he was uninhibited. I hated having to be what I perceived as the aggressor.

Phil and Gene were at opposite ends of the sexual spectrum. The truth was, I was much more compatible with Gene in that way—two Scorpios, oh my god, yes. Phil (a Virgo) had a major problem with intimacy, and Gene sometimes couldn't seem to get close enough.

But at first glance, one would think Phil and I were the perfect match—two misunderstood rebels, who lived their lives for music, both from a Jewish background; in fact, even from the same high school (Phil was Fairfax class of '63). We both were deeply concerned about the ills of the world and social injustice. Other than Native American issues, Gene hadn't seemed to express much of a strong opinion on those subjects, I had to drag it out of him. That perplexed me because he was so sensitive, but he wasn't exactly what you would call politically correct or even aware (despite the Dylan songs in his repertoire).

And though Sloan and I tallied up hours of what I perceived as meaningful conversations that seemed to change the Earth's axis, his problems went beyond anything I had ever encountered from someone professing to be completely sober. It was sadly driven home during our first public outing on July 4th, when he made an attempt to enjoy fireworks with me down at the beach. He couldn't handle it and had to leave abruptly, like a shell shocked war veteran, which in a sense, he was. And despite me playfully running circles around him in the sand and trying to make him laugh, I could see he was in a really grim place.

Earlier in April, we had shared the once in a lifetime viewing of Halley's Comet as it came around. It felt a bit weird taking Phil up to a place that had become sacrosanct to me and Gene, our spot high up above the coast near Ventura county line. Unfortunately, there were very few places away from the city lights where you could see the comet clearly. Phil described it as a smudged Q-tip in the sky, and he would write a song about it.

Later that night, we parked somewhere on the coast highway, with the ocean literally just outside. And it was on that night that Phil finally let loose. I remember him banging on the roof of the van.

I admit I did feel a twinge of guilt when I later went up on that hilltop to see the comet again, this time with Gene. Even though I had given Phil first dibs on the sighting, by the time Gene and I got up there, Halley's Comet was the last thing on our minds.

Later that summer, Phil gave me the proverbial "I need my space," and I took off to San Francisco for a few days to chill out. I sent him a psychedelic postcard from the Haight. I was beginning to think from his behavior, that he was just your atypical acid burnout from the '60s. Maybe that postcard wasn't a good choice? He said his drug days were well behind him, but it might have been his stories of how Barry McGuire used to spike his orange juice with acid.

Or the alternate story: that all of Phil's behavioral anomalies were merely a result of hyperglycemia. Okay. That was an interesting theory, but I still continued chalking up his alienation to years of mental illness and lack of social interaction.

Maybe it was bad timing (the story of my life), but Phil Sloan was looking for something I couldn't provide enough of, and try as I might, I couldn't be the scapegoat he was searching for. He needed something or someone to take away all responsibility for himself, to confuse free will with faithlessness, desire with ego. He needed to be told that his suffering had a grander purpose, in order to make it bearable. He needed to put a false optimistic face to his fatalism.

So he found a guru.

I came back from San Francisco to find that an old school friend of Phil's had introduced him to the world of Satya Sai Baba. Though the hairs on my neck didn't immediately stand up on end when I saw the picture of this East Indian guy, who looked like Hendrix in drag, I remember feeling decidedly queasy. Something was very, very wrong. And damn if I wasn't determined to save Phil from whatever it was!

13

"bend me, shape me, any way you want me...."

When Sloan and I first met, I would bring my guitar over to his apartment and we'd just doodle around. I really didn't intend for it to be more than that. In fact, he actually played a killer 12-string solo on the demo I was recording at the time, and even more importantly, wrote some of the chorus of one of the songs. Called "Horn of Plenty (The Ballad of Travis Petrie)", it was a treatise on the downfall of the American farmer, which we later submitted to Willie Nelson and Farm Aid. What Phil didn't know was that I was inspired to write that song, after a conversation Gene and I had had about the plight of rural communities in the middle part of the country, from whence he sprang.

It being the Reagan era, the corporatization of America was in full swing. So I was reading something in the news about foreclosed farms and farmers committing suicide. Though after submitting the song to Farm Aid, I never followed up on it. By that time, I was too far gone into these two relationships. Sadly, everything else in my life became secondary.

6 degrees: I was told by rock journalist Harvey Kubernik, brother of an old classmate from Fairfax High, to go take that demo to his buddy, Saul Davis—the one who just happened to be managing Gene at the time? Whose girlfriend, Carla, was recording with Gene? There I sat in Harvey's office over at MCA,

as he brought me up to date on what all his friend Saul was doing at the time.

I sat there looking Harvey straight in the eye, with the full knowledge I was secretly seeing Gene Clark and never said a word.

There's a reason why they say Scorpios make the best spies.

Phil Sloan, meanwhile, had never lost his ability to write, far from it. And his voice was in better form than ever (though he, like Gene and Nilsson before him, had a nasty smoking habit). It would blow my mind how he would sit down with his guitar, create an entire song out of mid-air, and then just as easily, let it fly away into the ethers never to be heard again. I briefly entertained thoughts of maybe having found a musical partnership with Phil, who definitely could use a catalyst to jump start his career, though I didn't approach Gene with that desire. He didn't need my help in that regard, for he had never stopped recording and had been consistently gigging for years.

That and because I was so intimidated by playing in front of him. Gene was so intense. All he had to do was look at me in a certain way, ambushing me with his eyes, and I'd melt into a pile of mush. I was falling so deeply in love with him, I couldn't even think straight, let alone remember lyrics. Add to that, the possibility that my 12-year-old inner child was going, "Oh crap, he's one of The Byrds," and I was rendered totally useless. I had played in front of the likes of Spencer Davis and shared a beer with Paul McCartney, but Gene Clark obviously affected me in a myriad of ways I did not expect.

I knew from my attempts at writing alone though, that I definitely needed the constant feedback and creative flow from another person, in order to feel complete. I really missed the creative dynamic I had for so long with Sandy. Deep down, I knew that would most likely never happen again.

What I didn't miss, was my old obnoxious competitive self, so when Phil's guru trip came along, I had the perfect excuse to drop everything and turn into Guerrilla Martyr Mary. I would fight to keep what I thought remained of Phil's sanity, playing on his acute intelligence and hoping he would see the light, whilst suffering the indignities of his repeated rejections, even just as a trusted friend. I was made to feel like an outsider in a world that I thought I was finally understood in. For me to overcompensate, I literally lost a part of myself in order to save him. It was probably just a convenient excuse for me to finally give up the ghost.

My guitar was put away in its case for a final time. I once told someone, "I used to be a musician."

They looked at me intently and said, "No—you're still a musician—you just aren't playing."

There I was again, on another mission to save a tortured soul from the '60s. I should have paid closer attention to the ex-girlfriend, who would call Sloan's apartment in tears, ad infinitum. A harbinger of things to come. His favorite mind fuck with women was, the more he rejected you, the more you would want to come back. I don't know how he twisted it around like that, but he was very good at it. I had wondered whether the ex-girlfriend had ever witnessed Phil talking to the imaginary little man on his shoulder, or writing song lyrics in crayon on the walls of his apartment, which he would completely rearrange, furniture and all, every few days.

In the Spring of 1987, I bought a 19-foot motor home that I named Diana, and took off to Flagstaff, where I volunteered for Big Mountain Support group on the Navajo 'rez'. It mostly entailed bringing supplies in from town and helping to herd sheep.

There is nothing so profound to connect oneself to the Great Spirit, than to smell burning juniper wood and to hear the pounding of tribal drums after midnight, under a starry dome in the middle of nowhere.

But fleeing to Arizona was not a simple act of altruism. My heart was also breaking from having to stay away from Gene for a while. Seeing him battle with the 'fire water' demon was starting to really get to me. It had been one thing to be friends or acquaintances with an alcoholic—quite another to be in love with one. He would show up drunk sometimes and be very scary, launching into that John Drew Barrymore impression that was anything but impressive. Just the fact that he would drive like that freaked me out. I begged him to just let me come get him when he was drunk.

He had tried to get me to ride on a motorcycle with him through Topanga Canyon. There was absolutely no way I would do that, having made the mistake once of letting him drive my poor VW bus. Even though it didn't seem to go over 45 miles an hour, I thought he would kill us both. "Aw, come on, mama, ride with me," he said playfully, with rather obvious sexual overtones. My comeback was choice.

"I'll ride with you, just not on that thing."

I had made the observation though that sometimes, the more length of time we were together, gradually his drinking would taper off. That spoke volumes to me. He was also trying to attend AA meetings, but told me it was like Catholic school, that he hated being preached to. At least he was trying, but then the withdrawal from the alcohol made him horrific to be around as well. I couldn't stand to see him suffering, but I realized that coming to me was his refuge. He certainly couldn't stay sober in the circles he was in.

But how could I make a difference in his life if I wasn't with him day to day? He didn't want me anywhere near the crazy scene at his house. And though he still created a beautiful picture of the life we could have up in Mendocino, he wasn't yet ready to set that in motion. Once again for me—a dream on hold.

So off I was, going to experience an entire community of Indians, leaving behind the one crazy part-Indian that I loved back in L.A. I didn't get the gist of that irony until years later, like so much else.

By this time, the *So Rebellious A Lover* album was finally being released, and I was hoping Gene would be okay for a little while, busy doing what he loved, and with more level- headed, sober, professional people around him.

We were not seeing each other as often as I wanted, but when we did, it was physically and emotionally exhausting for both of us, because we would play catch up for several days. Sometimes, we'd take off in the motor home. But more often, we'd hole up at a bungalow at the Topanga Ranch Motel on Pacific Coast Highway, which, just a few years later, was given Historical Building status. That is so priceless, they have no idea. If Gene hadn't been so sick by then, I think we would have both won a gold medal for sheer endurance.

Gene still said he wanted to find a way to break free from the other relationship, with the least amount of damage, but that co-dependent nightmare had been going on for years and it wasn't that easy. He was, at least to me, a very honorable man, not your typical rock and roll scoundrel by any means (though he could fake it really well). But after that gun incident at his house, I was freaked and he knew it. It worried me when he kept reiterating that he didn't want me to follow him to that dark place he was protecting me from.

What did he think he was going to do to me?

I had struggled with juggling the two relationships, even though they were so vastly different. I felt that I was living a double life, but so was Gene, who apparently decided to stay off and on with the drug dealer girlfriend, a decision that proved to be fatal in the long run.

Emotionally, I was already a wreck. I was faced with choosing between the profound intellectual connection and riffing word play that I dug with Phil (very similar to my friendship with Nilsson, I now realize), or the overwhelmingly impassioned and emotional bond I had with Gene. Both of them were keenly aware of some heavy duty karma going on, that's for sure— almost too consuming to describe. Each man offered me something I couldn't seem to live without and I didn't want to give either one of them up.

When I wasn't seeing enough of Gene, I knew it was because he was working. But when I wasn't seeing Phil, it was because he chose not to see me. *Big* difference. Either way it was a cruel waiting game. Phil would tell me not to wait for him, and Gene would say just the opposite!

I wasn't sure at the time whether Phil cared if I was in his life or not. He was constantly sending me mixed signals. He was what they call a 'crazy maker'. I would call him (because I *could*, you see), and he would hang up on me for no reason. I would go over to his apartment, knowing he was there, and he would totally ignore me and not answer the door. Crazy maker! I would find out years later, that he did this very same thing with several other women he was seeing at the same time. Talk about a double or triple life! Although, I should talk.

But Gene had shown in numerous ways that he cared, even in the midst of all the cloak- and-dagger stuff. We knew that we were just victims of circumstance and timing. I was grateful to still hear from him after I left for Arizona (as I had the same answering service), but I was careful always to guard my heart. Until it broke the next time.

Neither man ever found out about the other.

In the late autumn of '87, Gene's younger sister Nancy died tragically, from what he said were heart problems. I later learned she had a host of other problems, one of which afflicted her older brother. I would come to discover that several members of Gene's family had suffered from severe depression or mental disorders in varying degrees, some of them completely debilitated. It was something that Gene never talked about of course, maybe not even realizing why he was the way he was and the extent to which it was inherited, like the alcoholism that also ran in his family. But as he was telling me about his sister, I remember the fear in his face. By then, I was pretty good at reading him that way. And like so many other mysteries surrounding Gene, it's a case of, I wish I had known then what I know now.

Not long after that, Gene and I were at the Lamplighter, and even in the darkened bar, he looked awful. I just chalked it up to the drinking again, until he proudly showed me he was holding a club soda. I had no idea that within a few months, he'd be in a hospital, having a big chunk of his stomach and intestines taken out because of ulcers.

Key words to remember here are: ulcer and surgery.

I would see him taking antacids and Excedrin by the handful. Sometimes, he would even abruptly throw up, but I never made the connection. He just alluded to having a sensitive stomach, but he never told me what was causing all that pain and I would not find this out for 24 years. And since I wasn't looking for a scar, I never found one either. Gene orchestrated that perfectly too. Like a sleight of hand magician, he knew how to direct my attention to where he wanted it to be. He wasn't lying to me, he was just obfuscating and leaving out the details. He wanted to stoically create the illusion that he was just fine, I suppose. I would find out later that he did that same thing with certain friends and family.

We never made love in broad daylight in a shower again, that's for sure.

One night in 1988, during a fairly conventional movie date with Phil at the renown Chinese theatre on Hollywood Blvd., I happened to glance across the street to the historical Roosevelt Hotel and up to the marquee at the Cinegrill. Damn if it wasn't Johnny Rivers playing that night and sure enough, I made certain good ol' J.R. knew Sloan was there in the shadows, where he would reluctantly be brought up to do "Secret Agent Man". It had probably been decades since they'd seen each other and I looked at it as one of many peace treaties that I would set about, bringing to mend what I perceived as Phil's very broken heart.

I would do it again two years later with Papa John Phillips, who Phil had felt slighted by in 1967, during the initial meetings up at Phillips' house regarding the Monterey Pop Festival. According to Phil, when he showed up at the house, John shoved him up against a wall, holding a knife to his throat. He told Phil in explicit terms to split and to not dare show up at the festival. I never knew what that was all about or even if it was true.

What I did know was that the iconic guitar intro to "California Dreamin'" did not exist until Sloan came up with it one day and showed it to John Phillips—or so the story goes.

6 degrees: John certainly had his connection to Gene Clark, oh yes, he did. For Gene was the reason that John threw his wife Michelle out of The Mamas and Papas for a few months, back in 1966. Gene had been a bad boy on the sly before.

That reconnection in 1990 between Phillips and Sloan, was not quite what I had hoped for. John was playing with a new version of The Mamas and Papas (which included his actress daughter and apparent victim, Mackenzie) at a local club called At My Place in Santa Monica. I had been there for one of Gene and Carla's shows 3 years before.

I went down there alone. I called Phil from a pay phone and literally put John on the phone with him, where he convinced Phil to come down to the club. What I had foreseen as a really groovy night, reminiscing and talking music, degenerated into Phil talking about Sai Baba. My stomach sunk, as I could see John's eyes glassing over. It was a disaster, and all I could do was stand there and cringe, wondering why I still bothered.

Meanwhile, Gene was on the road again, and I was finding my jealous Scorpio mind filled with awful visions of what he might be indulging in with other women, especially if he was drunk. It was the late '80s and AIDS was still the big bugaboo. But I knew odds were that he would just end up in his hotel room alone or hang with some of the band. Gene's shyness had its benefits.

Still, he continued to sweetly think of me, calling from different stops along the way and leaving his funny little messages. He would call as Elvis (and oddly enough, Phil also had a spot- on Elvis impersonation; it's a generational thing).

I would in turn send Gene postcards from some of the places I was traveling; N.Y., Israel, London. I wanted to make sure I was still a stable constant in his life, no matter what else was going on. I would sign the cards 'J' or 'James'.

Just a couple of secretive Scorpios playing at covert lives— which may sound exciting, but the reality was devastating, at least to me. I now believe that Gene (and Phil as well) had to live in a state of constant longing in order to feed the muse. You know the tortured artist syndrome? But if they had to exist in that state, it follows that, so did I—whether I wanted to or not. I wrote a lot of anguished poetry during that time.

Gene's ongoing battle with alcoholism was still tortuous to witness. In the beginning, I was fairly naïve and didn't actually know what I was seeing when his hands would start to shake, or when he would lie next to me, sweating and shuddering. It was all I could do to wrap myself around his body and comfort him. At first, I thought it was some kind of nervous condition that I didn't want to draw attention to for fear of embarrassing him but then, the thought crossed my mind that maybe he was on heroin. I had seen *Panic in Needle Park*, I wasn't *that* stupid. So I started looking for tracks on his arms. There were none, so the only likely explanation were 'the DT's' as I later learned they were called.

Little did I know that Gene had actually been on heroin years before, and would be again. He didn't have to use a needle either.

The adventure with Phil meanwhile, had taken on an even more perilous turn than presenting him to former musical colleagues for their acceptance and forgiveness. In late June of 1989, I discovered I was pregnant. I had done the math and figured out, unfortunately, it wasn't Gene's (who would have been man enough to possibly react in a very different way than Phil did). By now I was 35 years old and the call of Motherhood was shrieking in my ears.

Phil had gone to India to grovel at the feet of Sai Baba yet again, and when he came back, he moved from yet another lonely apartment into his sister's house. I felt rather indignant about that prospect, so I went right over there, grabbed his toothbrush and some clothes, and took them with me to an apartment in Venice I had just found, two blocks away from the ocean. In essence, I kidnapped him. I must have been out of my gourd.

Phil and I lived together briefly for the first time but we were more like roommates. He stayed only a few weeks, for upon learning I was pregnant, went back to his sister's and launched into a campaign to have me abort our baby. He was 43 years old, had never been married, had never had children. *Big* red flags, all. I was bound and determined to bring into the world, what would be my only child. I started weighing my options.

I knew I was running some terrible risks, that Gene could either kill me, kill Phil or even worse, that I would lose him and have to live with the consequences.

But Gene didn't know where this new apartment was, and all I had was the message phone at first. I was surely out of my mind then, harboring a deep seated anger that I dare not voice. Gene had already had a family, his children were both nearly grown and here I was with nothing. What kind of a future was I looking at? I had to prepare for the possibility that I might just end up alone, with a baby.

And while I had believed in Gene's promises, I felt like he kept me hanging on, with a light at the end of a very distant tunnel. This new equation changed everything and called for desperate measures. I would deal with Gene when the time came—and if he really loved me, he would fight for me. I had seen him do it. Perhaps that was the lesson he was supposed to learn. Or was I just doing what I thought *he* had been doing all along at the Lamplighter—huddling there with me so perilously close to his house, where we could have been discovered anytime by the other girlfriend, thereby inviting the final Showdown at Gene's Corral?

Like him once sitting so tauntingly in the front row at a Mamas and Papas concert and ogling Michelle Phillips in full view of her husband? Gene seemed to court danger through the years in a multitude of ways. There again, who was I to talk?

I suddenly became responsible—because I had to be. Not only did I take full time work as a receptionist in a Malibu real estate office, but at night, started taking real estate classes (my mother was thrilled). I was exhausted, but my new schedule served as the perfect excuse when Gene finally saw my bedraggled self that early September day at the cove. I was not showing but I still never said a word.

We stayed our last night together at the Topanga Ranch and spent most of the night just watching PBS. He was not well at all—but neither was I.

The emotional stress of the job, the classes, and Phil's constant harassment over the situation, led to the 16th of September in 1989 where, just two days before Phil's 44th birthday, our baby boy was lost.

I named him Jesse Aaron.

Grief-stricken, desperately alone and facing a future that looked empty and meaningless, I checked myself into the Thalians Center at Cedars-Sinai Hospital. Phil never once came to see me. How I could even talk to him after that, I'll never know.

There is nothing quite like being in a place like that to make you realize just how very sane in comparison you really are. When I found myself being approached by the 'inmates' as if I were staff, I knew it was time to split. It started to look like a scene from *One Flew Over the Cuckoo's Nest*—catatonic people lining up for their meds with paper cups clutched in their shaky hands, shuffling down the hallways. Not for me, no thanks.

Though, just a year and a half later, those thoughts of suicide again came crashing down upon me—and for good reason.

14

"meanwhile, your fire is burning here"

Two months after losing the baby, I went to see Gene. I didn't care who was at the house, I desperately needed to be with him, especially after what I'd just been through. With him, I had been careful because he already had the two kids he couldn't take care of financially, and until he had made that decision for us, I didn't want to risk losing him by getting pregnant. It was a mystery as to how I got pregnant in the first place, as I was on birth control at the time. But I was not into playing that game of blackmail, no matter how overwhelming the desire was.

When Gene had talked of us leaving L.A., my shocking visions of being barefoot and pregnant by a wood stove in a little house in the woods was too much to bear sometimes, but that's precisely what I was dreaming about. So much for the liberated ex-lesbian.

I never told him that I had just lost another man's baby.

I was afraid of what I might find as I knocked on his door. We had been playing this game for so long by only his rules, and now I needed to take the risk of breaking them.

I stood back in hesitation when I heard the loud voices inside. Naturally it was all still goin' on over at Geno's, nothing had changed. Actually it had gotten worse. He had just received some major royalty money from Tom Petty having recorded "I'll Feel A

Whole Lot Better", and a bunch of his momentary buddies were already partying away at his expense.

When I finally saw Gene at the door, I realized right away that he was in trouble again. He was wild-eyed, drunk and terribly gaunt.

But just like ragged Captain Jack Sparrow, he was totally enchanting.

When he saw it was me, his whole demeanor changed. His face softened, he smiled and stepped outside, shutting the door behind him like a little kid on Christmas morning. But the smell of alcohol was overpowering and he looked like he hadn't slept for days. He proceeded to tell me how he couldn't find me, couldn't find my number. How could that be? He knew where to find everything in that house when he wanted to. My messages could have been intercepted.

He started begging forgiveness and at that point, I just fell apart and burst into tears. He sheltered me in his arms, once again my gentle protector. Had he even gotten my postcards? Why hadn't he said something? Were those intercepted as well?

He took me by the hand and we walked a few blocks from the house and stood near a streetlamp, silhouetted in light. We kissed and held one other for quite a while, just slowly rocking each other back and forth in a soothing rhythm. We didn't seem to say actual words for the longest time, because there was so much to say. He knew I was hurting bad. I knew he was hurting even worse.

I reached up to wipe the sweat from his face—or were they tears? Surely those were tears. It was cold out but he was soaking wet. I finally broke the silence and tried to make light out of our grim reality.

"Look at you, silly," as I buttoned up his Western shirt buttons against the autumn chill. I know I told him I loved him. He was an absolute beautiful mess.

I gave him the medicine bag I had made him for his birthday, containing a protective amulet, some herbs and a feather, always appealing to his Native spirit. I kissed him again, looking up into his eyes.

"Are you my Indian brave?"

He smiled, almost blushing, as he hemmed and hawed. He always seemed to love when I'd say that. He would play the role to the hilt.

"You're my good girl," he whispered, as if to reassure himself that I still was, stroking me like a pet, and kissing the top of my head. I pressed my body against him, trying to keep him warm. I could feel him slightly shivering. He told me he was still trying to get it together but that everything was just "so screwed up and crazy."

Looking at the shape he was in, I remember feeling a sickening urgency, like standing on the deck of the Titanic as it started to tilt.

I told him that it was time, that we really had to go and we had to go *soon*. What prompted me eerily to say that or an approximation of that, I'll never know. It was the closest I ever got to putting pressure on him.

Not yet, he said—the time wasn't yet right, that one day soon he would come for me, that we'd be free, he promised. He told me to keep the home fires burning—to keep "your fire burning." He said that his fire would still be burning for me.

I felt my heart pounding, with a lump in my throat and a deep, almost primal foreboding, like the sudden adrenaline rush when disaster is rushing headlong towards you and there's nothing you can do to stop it, nothing—but just to hold on tight, shut your eyes and wait for it.

I think I subconsciously shook my head in crushed disbelief, that Gene still did not have the faith he could finally leave the L.A. scene behind, then and there, and start anew. He'd had the courage to do it before. I wasn't asking him to give up his music, just to get the hell away from the very thing he was keeping me away from. Hadn't we been planning this for so long, almost since we met? Had he just been fantasizing and laying a trip on my head?

The timing was *so* right for me, I had absolutely nothing to stay for. But what was keeping him paralyzed there in that house, in a soul-numbing suburb covered in concrete, and where nothing could nurture his soul? Why was he still getting so messed up? He was a sitting duck with those people. As long as he kept opening the door to them, they'd keep coming. They'd take from him whatever they could and make sure to keep him fucked up just enough so the party would keep on going.

Gene was just too nice (or insecure) to say no. I just couldn't handle that insanity anymore, especially for what it was doing to him. I should have gone back to that house and thrown those vultures out of there, to risk losing him in order to save him.

If only I'd known.

I had a small, embroidered burgundy handbag with me that I still have to this day. I found a pen and a tattered piece of paper, then wrote my number down yet again and said something like "when you're ready."

Silently crying, I held his face in my hands, looked up into those piercing blue eyes longingly, one last time, caught my breath—and walked away.

He was still standing there under the streetlight watching me when I looked back. Did he think that he would never see me again? Did he know that I was still intending to wait for him? Or did he think I was abandoning him?

Those questions would haunt me for more than two decades. They still do.

Star-crossed tragic lovers, we were. A modern day Romeo and Juliet where the message got lost somewhere in translation, poison would take one lover and then the Fates would take what remained.

Everything Gene said to me that night, he wrote down in a song—"Your Fire Burning." I would not know the song existed until 2011—twenty-two years later.

The Cosmic Ranger's mighty wind stilled the flames—but he held on to one last match.

I gave up the apartment in Venice and moved into a building my mother owned in, of all places, Beverly Hills. I was about as out of place on Roxbury Drive as a Venice flower child could be. But the rent was free, I was grateful, and I stayed there in relative comfort, uncomfortably for the next three years. I was directionless, unhappy and looking for a place to feel validated, as time went by and I didn't hear anything from Gene.

The winter holidays came and went and I was devastated. I was hoping we would be taking in one of our humble traditions of going out to a place in Reseda called The Farm (sadly, gone), where they had pony rides and a petting zoo, with an old Western town motif. I had told Gene that I needed or wanted nothing more for Christmas than to see his face and sure enough, he managed to give me that. I knew he had no money, and me being the ultimate cheap date, we had been looking to do something together that was more in keeping with simpler pleasures. So for two Decembers, we went to the Farm.

I will never forget how he would talk to the goats, right up in their faces. He would engage them in this imaginary dialogue that just made me fall in love with him all over again. He had said that one day we would have goats of our own. Though he never talked about it much, I had wondered what he must have been like as a boy in Missouri on the family farm with animals around him, and the creek that ran near his house where he would catch what he called his 'mudpuppies'. It must have been a far off, happy, yet sad memory for him. Because once we left the Farm, he would get very quiet and pensive. There again was the silence that told a thousand tales.

So that Christmas, everything changed. I heard nothing from Gene for the first time in 4 years. Crushed, my faith in everything was fading fast.

Phil was never any good to be around during the holidays either. He didn't really enjoy anything, not even the times over the years when we would leave town and go to wonderful places, like San Francisco or Sedona. He always seemed to be weighted down in his head.

I also knew there was no place for me with him amongst the fanatical mindset of his new friends, the Sai Baba devotees. By this time, one of the Baba girls had designs on Phil and so I fought back in an unusual way. The more Hindu he tried to become, the more Jewish I became. It was a constant running battle. I went back to my roots for comfort, without ever having set foot in a synagogue.

I had gone to Israel on a search for self and meaning in the fall of '88, and it had a profound effect on me. However, the hardcore Jewish identity is so wrapped up in the concept of family, that to be alone in the scrutinizing midst of that only made me feel worse. I was just not 'synagogue singles dance' material, and I became even more isolated in the process of trying to fit in.

At the same time, I kept a door open to the pagan mysteries, and it was at a Women's Full Moon gathering in the Angeles Forest, that I met Blackbird. Of Native heritage, she was 16 years younger than I, but it was as if there was no difference at all. She became one of my best friends and my Grateful Dead traveling buddy. Over the next few years in the early '90s, we would hit the road in total Deadhead style, camping and partying along with the rest of the Dead's legendary legion of followers.

It wouldn't be the last time I would hit the road and dance my way through grief. Just another way to cope. I wish I had been hardcore enough to go to more shows when I had the chance. No one ever thought that particular long strange trip would end and I miss it even now.

Blackbird and I are still friends. She moved up to Bellingham, Washington where she too, went to work on a rez. Then she got into acting of all things. It was the same trip I had done in a roundabout way.

She's also one of only three people who have ever called me 'James'.

In November of 1990, Phil was honored by the National Academy of Songwriters at their 5th annual salute, held at the Wilshire Ebell Theatre. He performed for an audience of his peers (including Barry Mann and Cynthia Weil), and it was an incredible night where he held sway over the stage. He even received a standing ovation. I sat with Phil's sister Lynn and her son David. We were all extremely proud of him and I thought of how far he had come from the broken man I had first met.

As synchronicities go, it's hard to top the next one. My friend and Rabbi confidante, David Montag, had invited me to a Shabbat dinner high in the hills of Pacific Palisades, and who should I run into there but Phil's hero and The Byrds' favorite songwriter, Bob Dylan? Phil was not there to enjoy the coincidence as, in yet another twist, he finally got the spiritual roots bug and was on a pilgrimage to Israel.

His Bobness however, was going through another transformation at the time (having moved on from his Born-Again Christian period) and was trying to find some solace in the Chassid community, most notably the Breslov branch (who follow the teachings of Rebbe Nachman of Bratslav). He often hung out at the Palisades home of old Hibbing, Minnesota buddy Louis Kemp, who held wonderful Shabbat weekends, often with a guest speaker. I say he was *trying* to find solace because it was very evident to everyone there that night, that poor Mr. Zimmerman was very inebriated and it wasn't just from the Kosher wine at dinner. He had arrived that way.

Bob got very hostile and defensive with me in particular (naturally), and I can't even remember what was being said. But I had the distinct feeling he might not have wanted to hear anything from a woman at the table. Leave it to me to get in a heated argument with Bob Dylan. I ran into him a couple times after that (once, at the Chabad telethon) and he didn't seem to remember me or that night, which was a blessing.

My mother, Shirley (*) 1940s

My parent's star-studded wedding; with: Gabby Hayes, Robert Preston, Donald Richards, Milton Berle, John Howard, Mel Torme, Jerry Colonna and Morey Amsterdam (*) 1952

Dad and me (*) 1956

Outside my grandmother's house; Golden Beach, Florida (*) 1958

Me and Mom (*) 1961

My Beatle haircut; at the house in Benedict Cyn. (*) 1964

My "Juliet" period (*) 1969

The Skiffles (*) 1971

Me and my cherished 1965 Epiphone Casino (*) 1971

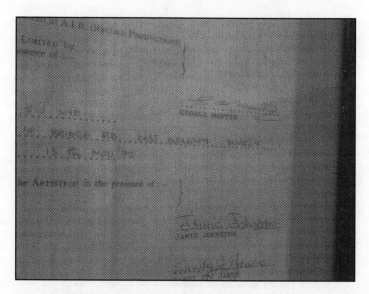

The record contract with George Martin (*) 1972

Complete transformation (*) 1976

Another transformation; Actor's Studio, L.A. (*) 1981

"The real Gypsy Rider"; Appleby Horse Fair, Cumbria, England (*) 1984

My first heart dog, Gypsy (*) 1987

My beloved Gene; Sherman Oaks, CA (Henry Diltz) 1983

P.F. Sloan and me, Santa Monica, CA (*) 1990

My roots tour; Annandale, Scotland (*) 1992

Me and Barry McGuire, just a-gettin' higher (*) 1992

Surfer girl's dream come true; with Don Murray (Gayle Fann) 1994

My Billie; 40th anniversary of Summer of Love, S.F., CA (*) 2007

The day I got Chico; NorCal Aussie Rescue,
Grass Valley, CA (Kim Kuenlen) 2008

My beloved step-father Jack Wells, in the studio (*) (I'm guessing, 1980s)

The end of the long road to Tipton, MO (Photo
Credit: Laura N. Hoover) 2011

Our booth at the Lamplighter, augmented some (*) 2012

The first picture of Rick and me; McCabe's, Santa Monica, CA (*) 2013

Jamie and Rick today (*) 2017

15

"power to the people, right on"

For most of my life, I had believed in the power of the individual to change what was wrong in society. I hadn't been a fanatical cause junkie, but I did my part when presented with a chance to participate in things I believed in, to make a difference.

During my time in San Francisco from '77-80, I was very involved, be it with gay issues or even walking precincts for Ted Kennedy's 1980 presidential campaign. There had been the years following that where I had participated in anti-Contra rallies and various Alliance For Survival anti-nuke events around the L.A. area. Of course there was the afore-mentioned time with Big Mountain Support Group on the Navajo reservation. And along with my reluctant activist friend Phil Sloan, who just happened to write the quintessential protest song of all time, there would be several events we were involved in that made me feel good that we were contributing something positive together. It was what I had envisioned our relationship would be when we first met. Once again, I had organized all of his appearances at these events.

In December of 1989, there was the Heal the Bay rally in Santa Monica, where Phil had come face to face with Brian Wilson for the first time in over 20 years. I got the distinct feeling both men were seeing each other's ghosts.

On Earth Day, April 22, 1990, Phil performed in front of an enthusiastic crowd in Santa Barbara, along with Kenny Loggins and Jackson Browne, who were sharing the bill that day. Jackson, when told it was P.F. Sloan whose hand he was shaking, just dropped his jaw and went "Oh wow." Apparently Jackson was one of those people that thought Sloan was just a character in a Jimmy Webb song.

In January of 1991, with the Gulf War in full swing, Phil and I were down at the Federal building in downtown L.A. at an anti-war rally, where he got up on stage with Graham Nash and Ron Kovic (*Born on the 4th of July*), and did an apropos updated version of "Eve of Destruction" that blew everybody away.

I was so busy running around trying to save the world, I had no awareness of the fact that, at that very moment, The Byrds were being inducted into the Rock and Roll Hall of Fame at a gala held at the prestigious Waldorf Astoria Hotel in New York. Gene was actually there, along with the other four Byrds. It was the last time the five men would ever be together again.

Yes, it was good to be busy, involved in things that had meaning.

It's probably what saved my life, when I learned on May 24th of 1991, on my brother KC's birthday and Bob Dylan's 50th birthday, that Gene had been found dead at the house in Sherman Oaks.

He was just 46 years old. They said it was from 'natural causes'.

I can't remember now if it was on TV or the radio, all I remember is the sound of my own scream, and then sliding down the side of my bed to the floor, where all I could do was shake uncontrollably and sob. I curled up in a fetal position and stayed there for what seemed a very, very long time. I don't remember anything for days after that.

Natural causes. Too simple for a man so complex. I couldn't quite believe that, and a million other horrific scenarios went flashing through my head. But there was no one I could call, no one I could ask. I had to stop myself from rushing over the hill to the house. I realized there could be press there and it wasn't a good idea, because I would no doubt be hysterical.

105

There was no comfort for me anywhere, so I chose to stay invisible and bury my grief. Not just at that moment but for another two decades. Even my best friend Dena did not know about Gene. She thought all my tears had been for Phil when much of the time, I was crying for Gene. He was very much locked away in my heart, my most cherished secret. Dena told me years later, in her wonderful country wisdom—the deeper you love, the tighter you hold it in your heart. She understands now why I couldn't speak of Gene. It was almost as if I feared just the utterance of his name would be something I could not survive.

It took me a full 20 years later, in 2011, to find out what really happened or at least what various people had alluded to in the Einarson book. It also took 20 years for me to finally face my guilt over forcing myself to stay away from Gene, to make a choice during those 18 months.

When I didn't hear from him after that night under the street light, I knew there was something terribly wrong when he couldn't even call. Funny how I didn't feel betrayed. I knew it must be that he did not want me to see what was happening to him. I knew that much. Gene was ever so proud.

But had I known how bad it had gotten over at that house, how quickly he was spiraling down, I would have broken the door down to get him out of there. But I didn't know. Not then.

I always left him a forwarding number, even if I had to drive over to the valley and leave a piece of paper in an envelope under the door or in the mailbox, just saying 'J' and the number. I had done that very thing as soon as I had moved to Roxbury. Sometimes I didn't even know if it got to him, which was why perhaps for a time, he said he couldn't find me. But I couldn't go after him again. He promised he would come for me. I wanted him to be the one to make that final move. He had to for his own sense of manly pride.

And despite the way it looked sometimes, Gene didn't use people—people used Gene. He had a pure generous heart and would give you the proverbial shirt off his back. And that is how so many people could take advantage of him. Despite the insurmountable alcohol and drug problems that plagued much of his life since the '70s, he was still honest to the core, and an incurable old-fashioned romantic. I truly believed that one day he would, indeed, make good on his promise and come back for me.

Alas, he never did. At least, not from this side of the veil.

I remembered the time Gene had come to me after having had another fight with the other girlfriend. He was clearly upset, pacing like a caged animal, as he was sometimes wont to do. He had that look on his face, like, at any moment, he could smash something. I had seen it before when he threw one of my lamps against a wall.

But this time, he aggressively pinned me down on the bed, held my wrists and looked into my eyes and said, in an almost threatening way, "You wouldn't ever leave me, would you?"

"Never," I said.

"You mean that?"

And I told him, I meant it with all my heart and soul. How was it then, that he ended up leaving me? He may not have meant to. He just may have been sidetracked by certain people that showed up back in his life at that moment and took advantage of his weaknesses. I have to believe that's what happened.

I now know the names of some of those people and I know where they are—the ones that are still alive.

Gene's sense of time may have definitely been distorted, but mine wasn't. The time passed and it passed. And while I kept myself busy—Gene finally ran out of time.

I waited for him—as he had asked me to. I waited for 18 months.

All I have left from Gene, is a beautiful Indian silver turquoise and coral ring, that he gave to me in the late summer of 1986. He didn't make a big deal about it but still, I was stunned, all the while trying to act cool. Once he saw it fit precisely on my ring finger, he seemed pleased with himself, head nodding—a very satisfied smile on his face.

In retrospect, it was almost as if he were branding me. As if he were leaving an everlasting bookmark in the pages of my life.

It is the only ring I have ever received from a man. But after he died, I put it away in my jewelry box and would not speak of Gene or listen to his music, for the next 20 years.

Reeling from grief, thoughts of suicide left me paralyzed for I don't remember how long after that. But my mother being alive, that was always the spanner in the works. I couldn't do that to her. So as I was to do throughout my life when faced with overwhelming grief, I took advantage of the first opportunity I had to get the hell out of there—and I hit the road.

When Rabbi David came up with a spur of the moment trip to Santa Cruz, I jumped right into his coffee cup-strewn van. Of course, he had invited Sloan to go along as well (just my luck), so off we all went, like three Merry Pranksters.

I was to perform one of the better acting jobs of my life when we stopped through Ojai on the way north, and I was painfully reminded of the precious time there with Gene. But David really kept me together on that trip. He was such a glorious light unto the world anyway. He always made me laugh at the tiniest things. His usual pronouncement on the most mundane moments of good fortune was often: "It's a miracle!"

That last minute sojourn was just what I needed, but when I came back to L.A., a deep depression set in. I needed to throw myself into something to survive, anything that could keep me from drowning in despair.

Thank goodness for the 1992 Jerry Brown Presidential campaign. I walked in there prepared to merely stuff envelopes and ended up becoming the Assistant to the Director of Environmental Issues, which entailed—stuffing envelopes.

They also needed someone to be the Official Bard of the Campaign and as luck would have it, Mr. Brown, the former 'Governor Moonbeam' of California, was very impressed with the legendary protest ditty that Phil had written back in 1965. One of his favorite songs, said the Governor. Before we knew it, we were on the college campaign trail, with Phil singing his songs for hundreds of college kids, and me taking pictures from behind the stage, overlooking a sea of responsive faces.

6 degrees: One of the events we participated in was held at the Santa Monica Airport, where there was a huge fundraising concert. Who should perform but Gene's old Byrd mate, David Crosby (along with Graham Nash)? I took a picture of the Croz with his wife Jan, and Phil is smiling rather reluctantly behind them. Strange days, indeed.

Of course, Jerry didn't make it to President (a sax playing dude from Arkansas did), but instead went on to become the Mayor of Oakland and Governor of California again for a third time. Not too shabby a gig after all.

In November of '92, my friends Christopher Hill and his lady Angela came over from London to catch up with some old friends, one of whom was renown keyboardist Nicky Hopkins. It was another one of those times when I just kept quiet, because to do otherwise would have opened up a whole world of hurt. Thus, I never mentioned to Nicky or his wife Moira, that Nicky had been playing in Gene's band when we met at the Central that January night in 1986, a lifetime ago.

Nicky would die in 1994, only two years later in Nashville, from complications after intestinal surgery, something I would come to know too much about later in life. His wife Moira and I kept in touch, and I finally told her about Gene one day, while chatting on Facebook.

Chris Hill was a bloke who knew everybody, having worked at the Indica Gallery back in the day when John met Yoko there. He went on to work for McCartney and Wings, and then with Denny Laine. On that trip to the States, Chris took me and Denny Laine's oldest son, Damian, out to visit his friend and Eric Clapton's old band mate Ginger Baker, who was at that time, living 70 miles north of L.A. out in Lancaster, keeping polo ponies! I remember Ginger had what appeared to be a pet black widow who lived in a window near his fireplace. And there were an assortment of rather large dogs, that looked to be an amalgam of Irish wolfhounds, Great Danes and Gypsy lurchers.

Earlier in the summer of '92, I had gone back to London one more time and stayed with Chris and Angie, who were living not far from Camden Town where my old friend Leonard Whiting was living. It was the last time I saw Leonard. We took one last stroll on Primrose Hill. He ended up getting married again and we pretty much lost touch after that.

One night, we went to see Stevie Wonder perform and Chris took me backstage. There was Eric Clapton, standing in a circle of people. I had never seen Clapton play live so this was the best I could do. And meeting Ginger Baker just a few months later was a total trip.

Another London friend, Earl Okin, a thoroughly unique singer-songwriter with a penchant for vintage jazz and bossa nova, who had once opened for McCartney and Wings during their 1979 tour, was playing the Edinburgh Festival that August. I deemed that to be the perfect excuse for me to finally do the roots thing, and check out where my father's people had come from.

It turned out there was a Johnston Museum in a town called Moffat in Dumfries and Galloway, not far from Lockerbie where Pan Am 103 went down in 1988. My nearest relative, the 11th Earl of Annandale and Hartfell, still lived in the family castle. I actually found a number for him in a local phone book, called him up and told him I was a Johnston visiting from California. I don't think he was too amused.

While back in London, I spent a good deal of time running with my old friend Jo Jo Laine, who still had the flat she and Denny used to live in on the High Street in St. John's Wood. Jo Jo was gorgeous, vivacious and a little bit over the top in so many ways, but I loved her. She was an impetuous, but sentimental Cancer, who cherished her family and always kept a beautiful home. A nice Catholic girl brought up in Boston, she had the distinction of having lost her virginity at seventeen, to Jimi Hendrix at Woodstock in 1969! She went on to have trysts with Jim Morrison and Rod Stewart, amongst others. Even with all the rock stars I had encountered along the way, my experiences couldn't hold a candle to hers, not that I was trying to.

Jo Jo was now being tagged by the London tabloids as one of several 'wifelets' to the eccentric Alexander Thynn, the

7th Marquess of Bath. Alexander was a weekend warrior in the 'traveler convoy', partaking, as I had done, of the summer music festival scene and often camping in a tee pee. Jo Jo and I and her two kids, Laine and Heidi, camped also at one of those festivals, Elephant Faire in Cornwall.

Where Alexander actually lived, was at Longleat House in Wiltshire, a stately manor set on 10,000 acres and built by Sir John Thynne in 1579. Many of Alexander's amazing painted murals covered the ceilings. He also created the elaborate hedged mazes on the property. Longleat also boasted the very first safari park outside of Africa, which opened in 1966.

My sweet friend, actress Lisa Cavanaugh, another damaged Catholic girl from Boston, had joined our little party at Longleat. I had met Lisa after having just returned from England, in late December 1984, whilst doing the play *The Acting Teacher* at a theatre up on Hollywood Blvd. She was another one of those people in my life that had substance abuse problems and was in and out of twelve-step for years. I hated to see what she was going through but she was also the one person I had considered telling everything to about Gene, because I thought she would understand his disease and my heartbreaking battle to help him. But she was already knee deep in stories about my crazy dance with Phil, so I didn't want to complicate matters.

Besides, Lisa knew too many players in the L.A. scene and it was too risky. If word had gotten back to Gene that I had betrayed his confidences, it would have been over.

Lisa had her own relationships with a few rock musicians; Steve Jones of The Sex Pistols for one. But it was her liaison with Marlon Brando's son Christian, during the time he was implicated in the murder of his half sister's boyfriend, Dag Drollet, that made things get really scary for Lisa. So she fled back to Boston to have the baby daughter that Marlon would mysteriously take a real shine to whenever she came back to visit L.A.

By 1993, Phil and I were edging closer and closer to the last year of our turbulent and ever fascinating relationship. After more than 20 years, he would finally record his first full length album at a studio up in Seattle. By then, he was back living in Venice where I so wanted to be.

Thus, I stupidly moved from my mother's spacious two-bedroom luxury apartment building in Beverly Hills, to Phil's much smaller functional one-bedroom in what was close to the Oakwood area of Venice, more known at the time for its gang activities than art galleries.

One of the last memories I have of that apartment on Roxbury, was the day Phil and his sister Lynn showed up with Barry McGuire! It was the first time I would meet McGuire after all the many years of 6 degrees (which of course started with him being *the* face of The New Christy Minstrels, during the time Gene was in the group). Somebody took a picture of him giving me quite the bear hug, which is apropos because he was quite the bear.

I believed that finally, after all those years of struggle with Phil, that our life might miraculously and triumphantly be coming together, as he was all I had left. He would call me from Seattle and tell me about his day in the studio. I was so pathetically optimistic. I thought surely this meant something, even though once again, we lived more like roommates than lovers. How naïve and silly was I, grappling at straws blindly in the dark.

It lasted all of six months. With the album done and the production team up in Seattle shopping it around to no avail, Phil's mood started to turn ugly again and I was out on my ass.

More specifically, I decided to go up to Seattle myself on an invite from a dear old actor friend who was living there, and he dared me to come up and read for a part in *Northern Exposure*. I was a big fan of the show and Patrick assured me with his contacts and my required quirkiness as an actor, I would slip right in. He was right.

Despite my separation anxiety from Phil and home, I settled right into life in the Great Northwest, sippin' my lattes and diggin' the trees. I got my audition on the show, even got a call back. It looked real good. But the thought of nine months of impending rain made me turn tail and run home, after only a few months.

Not only that, it was a phone call to the apartment back in Venice that scared the shit out of me and made my stomach sink with a sickening rollercoaster drop. Some crazy fuck calling himself Dr. Z, had planted himself into Sloan's life and was acting as his 'spiritual attorney'. And the moment I had this nutcase on the phone talking about a crystal he had gotten from the Space People, I knew everything had rapidly descended into utter chaos and insanity in my absence. I should have stayed away and left Phil to his fate.

Instead I walked directly into madness.

16

"you know something's happening
but you don't know what it is...."

I dumped a brand new rented apartment in Bellevue, Washington, packed up the car and jammed back down to L.A. within a day and a half. I did not pass Go and went directly to Hell.

No one was there at the apartment when I arrived, yet the back gate was unlocked and the sliding glass door leading into the apartment was wide open. What I saw was worse than anything even Hunter S. Thompson could have left in his wake. The garden looked like it had been the epicenter of some demonic ritual, with bowls scattered all over the ground and everything in disarray. Inside, the apartment itself looked even worse. Stuff was strewn around all over the place and there were bowls and cups filled with rotten food all over the floor. The coffee pot was on and the smell of burnt coffee permeated the place.

This was so *not* Sloan, whose Virgoness manifested itself in the utmost tidiness. I looked around the room, felt nauseous and broke out into a cold sweat. The negative vibe in the place, washed over me like some maniacal monsoon.

Then I heard the back gate open and voices. I went outside and was confronted by this dark, bearded, mad-eyed stranger that looked like one of Manson's minions. And while Phil just stood

114

there sheepishly looking on, this guy who I perceived to be Dr. Z, proceeded to attack me verbally, even threatening me physically by jutting out his chest and aggressively coming towards me.

I realized again with utter devastation, just how different Phil was from Gene, for Gene would have never allowed someone to treat me like that. He would have been on that guy in five seconds flat.

That experience left me totally shaken to the core. I was certain that now I knew the reason for the negative portrayal of burned out people left over from the '60s. This guy was a first rate psycho. He had told Phil that he had been Jerry Garcia's physician (oh yeah, right), and a host of other bullshit stories that kept my gullible friend on the hook.

Meanwhile, Phil had been scheduled to do a hugely important media blitz 'comeback' performance, debuting the new album at the renown Troubadour in West Hollywood. It should have been P.F. Sloan's majestic return to the overground world of music he had been kept away from for decades. He should have taken back the time stolen from him. Instead, it was the worst case scenario—he takes up with a con artist who moves in with him, who then takes him to Hawaii for a week and plies him full of acid, just before a hugely important make or break show. This is what Phil had originally told me about that trip to Hawaii, but later of course, he denied it—the acid part I mean.

The industry came and the industry went. Sloan had blown it big time. Even though he performed well, he allowed Dr. Z and his entourage to make a fool of him *onstage*! And since he was treating me like a pariah and not listening to anything I had to say, there was no one there for a reality check. Through the years, if nothing else, Phil could always count on me as a friend to tell him the truth. It would always stun me silly when he didn't trust me, as time and time again I was right.

Dr. Z (whose real name turned out to be Ron) left Phil's life, career and his phone bill in shambles. Phil's moment to take back what was lost had come and gone, and all I could do was sit on the sidelines and watch it all float away, like the songs he so easily created to let fly into the ethers. By then, Phil was close to 50 years old. I knew he would most likely not be given another chance and may never be taken seriously again, at least not in this unforgiving town.

Two days before the Northridge earthquake in January of 1994, I got word that my old intellectual sparring partner, Harry Nilsson, had died. The only reason I ended up at his funeral was thanks to rock journalist Dawn Eden, who had invited me. The last time I had seen Harry was in March of '89, and that was a total accident.

I had been out at dinner with my folks at Mason's (now Pecorino) in Brentwood. Mason's was owned by James and Pamela Mason's son Morgan, who is married to Belinda Carlisle of The Go Go's. I have a picture of Harry and I from that night only because my stepfather Jack, happened to have a camera. It's not a very flattering picture of Harry, who had gained a shocking amount of weight.

I stupidly had invited Phil to accompany me to Harry's funeral, as I figured many of his peers would be there. And many *were* there; Paul Williams, Van Dyke Parks, and the illustrious Jimmy Webb who, in 1971, had written the aforementioned tribute song "P.F. Sloan", that was originally recorded by The Association and later by Jackson Browne.

But Phil wouldn't go and in the ensuing years, created this incredibly cockamamie story, whereby I suggested he go to the funeral to meet George Harrison, so he could get a record contract! Excuse me? How would I know George Harrison would even be there? It was, in fact, Ringo that had been Harry's best running buddy for years (after Lennon died). Maybe when I told Phil that indeed, Harrison *had* been there (and Phil had been trying to connect with him, someone he saw in the business as having 'spiritual credentials'), that he concocted this tale.

Just another one of Phil's justifications for his innate low self-esteem. It really hurt my feelings and left me astounded that he would think I could be so cold and calculating. This was a funeral for someone that I had known and loved. And my inviting Phil to

Harry's funeral, was my way of telling Phil, that he himself should be elevated to that height of songwriting status.

Disgusted by that whole scenario, I felt the cosmos was telling me to regroup, but how and where? I had returned from Seattle with nowhere to go. I desperately needed safety, saneness and balance around me. Gene was dead and Phil was a dead issue.

I ended up temporarily moving into a supposed vegetarian community, in a Venice house I saw advertised in the paper. It only took me a couple weeks to realize—it was a facade for a Rajneesh commune! Oh wonderful. It could only happen to me. By then deceased, Rajneesh's followers had started calling him 'Osho' (as if we wouldn't figure it out eventually). They had dispensed with the trademark red and orange clothing, which is why it took me so long to suss it out.

After a month under their roof, I moved into the back room of an art gallery on the Venice boardwalk, overlooking the ocean and run by an acquaintance of mine, a lady I knew from the 'frum' (Orthodox) community. She needed someone to help manage the gallery and it sounded really groovy and just what I needed. Unfortunately, she wasn't as organized as I was so nothing much got done.

I was basically in a haven from the storm until there was a lull. The good part of this arrangement was that I went to a lot of art galleries and receptions, and even saw my ex-partner Sandy occasionally, who had gone back to her first love of art and was studying at the prestigious Otis Parsons. I kept as busy as I could and saw Phil less and less, as I struggled to gain a sense of balance and do some serious soul searching. It is no wonder that the search I was on that Spring of 1994, led me to something that would totally transform my life for the next 18 years. From out of the deep blue it came—and who would have believed what it was?

11

"let's go surfin' now, everybody's learnin' how...."

I honestly don't know what possessed me at the age of 40, to suddenly pick up a little piece of shitty polyethylene foam that barely came up to my bellybutton, and try to ride it in a wave. But in all the years I kept being drawn back to Venice Beach, it never dawned on me that there might be something else for me out there, something magical hidden just beneath the surface, beckoning like a mermaid's whisper on the wind. And that seed that had been planted back in the early '60s in elementary school, was just now starting to sprout.

The distant strains of The Chantays' "Pipeline", The Sandals' "Endless Summer" and finally the words of "Surfin' Safari" that would not leave my head as I stared out at the ocean that Spring. It was time.

I had heard the call of a true bliss.

I started surfing. Specifically, bodyboarding (known as 'boogie boarding' to the landlocked), which is a sport passionately predominated by 15-year-old boys whose thrill in life is risking a snapped neck, by getting slammed down onto the shore from steep drops at places like the Wedge in Newport Beach or Zuma Beach in Malibu. That isn't my style. I was at heart, a longboarder

118

in a bodyboarder's shorts. Old school prone riding down the line, no gnarly maneuvers, just some simple carves and cutbacks and I am in heaven.

In 1994, I was usually the only female in the water and most definitely the oldest.

It began back then with that simple crappy beginner's board, one without a slick bottom (which immediately points you out as a kook; that and not using fins). You know, the kind you see tourist kids dragging down the beach by their leashes like reluctant terriers. By summer, I had graduated to a $50 Morey board from Target, with a semi-slick bottom that I had bought for its bitchin' purple and turquoise swirly design (what a girly thing to do). From there I went to a sweet BZ board with channels. I eventually would go to work for the guy who designed that board, Ben Severson.

I joined the Surfrider Foundation and started finding myself glancing through surfing magazines, until I finally subscribed to a publication strictly for bodyboarding. I quickly re- learned all the vernacular of the sport and found to my surprise that some words had survived through the years since my childhood—words like 'tube', 'stoked' and 'bitchin'. Some words had been transformed slightly; 'gremmie' was now 'grommet' or 'grom'. But for the most part, the surf rats that I hung with when I was ten were still basically the same.

With one major exception—their music.

In the surf shops, I noticed the surf videos had soundtracks to them that were predominantly punk or thrash metal. It was totally wrong, glaringly out of place with the feeling I personally had when I was in the water. To me, the ocean and surfing was nearly a spiritual practice—a form of meditation at times. I started to remember the music from the early '60s that complimented so many of the surf movies I had seen then. Where did it go, that "Endless Summer?"

Obviously, the British Invasion had squelched it instantly upon its arrival. The Beach Boys—well, they kind of evoked the mood I was looking for. So it was off to the second hand record stores to scout around for some bargain Beach Boys tapes. Those and compilations I found with corny titles, such as *Surfin' Hits* and *Surf's Up, Dude!* would have to do. I discovered that the ones that had predominantly instrumental tunes on them were the ones that affected me the most. That should have been a clue.

Since I had been living in a tiny room in the back of the gallery, and there were strangers coming in and out at all hours, I was feeling extremely vulnerable. So I took a single apartment alone, again overlooking the Venice boardwalk. It was affordable then and I could still see and smell the ocean. That was all I needed. Or so I thought.

Phil always seemed to get more miserable around summer and break up with me (and this from the man who wrote "Summer Means Fun"). This summer was no different. By mid-August and with the coming autumn, I was so tired of the prospect of facing yet another set of holidays alone, I couldn't stand it. I was angry and felt cheated by life. With my music career gone, my acting career barely even a joke, I still had absolutely no direction or goal. Surfing was all that mattered and this Beverly Hills princess-cum-ex-rock and roller, was quickly becoming a beach bum.

All I needed then was a miracle.

The Santa Monica Pier was a peripheral landmark throughout my life, even though I grew up in the canyons, miles away from the beach. But I would see it as a kid, whenever I would go down to the gone, but now legendary, Pacific Ocean Park (fondly known as POP). I would see it whenever I would hop a bus to spend the day walking around the arcades and riding the merry-go-round there. I had taken buses down there to watch the filming of *The Groovy Show* in the late '60s. It had gone through years of disrepair and several facelifts, but the postcard perfect welcoming arch that rode high above the entrance to the pier, remained the same for as long as I could remember. You could even see the sunset through it on many a summer evening. It looked just the way I remembered it, on that warm August 18th in 1994—when I met Don Murray.

My miracle had arrived.

18

"do you believe in magic...?"

What was it that possessed me that evening to go see Dick Dale and The Surfaris, for the Twilight Dance Series on the pier? The search for a soundtrack to the lifestyle I had suddenly found myself in? I had very little memory of Dick Dale, and the only memory I had of The Surfaris, was priding myself on being able to play "Wipeout" on my desk as a kid, better than anyone else. So I had never seen either artist. By the time I was watching TV shows like *Shindig* and *Hullabaloo*, it was the British invasion bands and their American counterparts that I paid attention to. Bands like The Turtles. A band that my ex-boyfriend Phil Sloan had written three big hits for.

So imagine my shock when they announced from the stage that the drummer of The Surfaris was Don Murray, the original drummer from The Turtles! Well, well I said. I really should go introduce myself. The P. F. Sloan connection was just way too much of a 6 degrees to overlook.

After their set, I went to the fence surrounding the stage and asked someone to go get Don. He came from behind the stage, and through the fence, we saw each other for the first time. I looked into his twinkling hazel eyes and a smile that shook the evening chill off my lightly clad sun-kissed skin. Though I couldn't

121

help but notice he was not too thrilled to hear Phil's name. I didn't know why at the time.

I hung around that night for quite a while as the band packed up, mostly talking to the leader of The Surfaris, Jim Pash, who oddly enough was very into ancient Jewish music. I mean *really* ancient, as in, the Harp of David. Don later told me that he was fascinated and impressed that I could keep up with Pash's conversation on the subject. I left that night with an invite from Jim to come for a lesson on the harp so I got his card.

Two months later on October 17th, lonely and not wanting to go back to a nine-year nowhere relationship, I remembered the twinkling hazel eyes and that devastatingly beautiful smile, so I called Jim Pash to get Don Murray's number.

Now *I* was the one calling to get a number.

I knew nothing about conventional dating. I knew nothing about how to 'hook' a man. All I knew is that from the moment Don Murray and I spent a day together, walking around Venice Beach and talking for hours, I felt completely and utterly myself. I felt happy and alive again. It was only when I allowed myself to feel guilt over leaving a relationship that was obviously over, but that I had invested so many years in, that the trouble began.

In the beginning of life with Don, I broke his heart. I was overly cautious. But he had a sweet and open-minded clarity about how he perceived my character. He said that any woman who could walk away that quickly from such a long relationship without any remorse, was a woman that couldn't be trusted. That she could easily do that to him. His was such a thoroughly Scorpio way of thinking (praising utterly stupid loyalty, even in the face of total self- destruction), that my own Scorpio heart just opened like a rosebud in bloom.

Yes—another Scorpio man. The Cosmic Ranger sure didn't miss a beat.

That was the turning point for me. That and Don almost leaving to take a job in Las Vegas, when Phil suddenly turned around and, having now bought a house for the first time, made it look like he wanted me back. Boy, I nearly fell for it too.

But no. I chose life with this glorious miracle of a man, who would share intimate little home cooked meals with me, and watch *The X Files* with me, and make love to me nearly every day in a tiny single termite-ridden apartment in Venice, where gunshots could be heard a block away, but where the ocean was our front yard. A man who cherished me as I was, who would take my hand protectively as we strolled along the Boardwalk, as if we had been waiting to do that all our lives. A man who would make me laugh aloud and never cry, except when he said how much he loved me.

And the day he asked me to marry him.

That was only a month or two after our very first date (at the Cafe '50s in Venice, where Don so chivalrously cut the last onion ring in half).

And you know how all of a sudden, you see your life becoming your Life? That who you are at that moment is the person that is finally real and definable? I had felt that way only once before when I was nineteen and got that record contract. I thought—this is it. This is who I am. For the rest of my life.

Well—remember what I said about something being too good to be true.

I eventually found out why Don had such a remote look on his face when I first met him and told him I had been P.F. Sloan's girlfriend.

Thirty years earlier, the two then 20-year-olds, nearly had a knock-down drag-out fight in the studio over a particular drum solo on a Turtles recording of one of Phil's songs, "You Baby". Don wanted to do a thoroughly original syncopated drum beat, that had never been used on a pop record. Phil objected and suggested they use the biggest session drummer of the time, Hal Blaine. Don went nose to nose with Phil and said, "No, we play on our *own* records" (my goodness, was that a dig at The Byrds, who hadn't all played on their first record)?

Phil went storming out, and somebody said to Don, "Well, there goes your songwriter. Go after him."

But Don stood his ground. "I'm not going after him," he said proudly.

Decades later, that syncopated drum beat was used on every rap record there was.

Here's another little interesting tidbit, filed under the 6 degrees folder: when Don left The Turtles in 1966, he was replaced briefly by a guy named Joel Larson. Joel had been the drummer for The Grass Roots (the band so closely associated with P.F. Sloan; in fact he created them) and then, (drum roll, please)—The Gene Clark Group! In fact, it was Joel who was playing with Gene during that 1966 stint at the Whisky, where I had espied Gene walking in through the club's side door!

By 1994, Don hadn't been on a surfboard in 22 years. Though he had been one of those tousled-headed bleached blondies amongst the hordes of young California boys, living and breathing surfing in the pre-Beatle '60s. When it became uncool to be identified with anything surf, especially if you were in a band, he just stopped. But that surfer persona never left him. He walked the walk (more like a cool glide) and talked the talk. He was the only grown person I had ever met that still used the word 'bitchin'. Though he buried that persona for years, living with various women who didn't appreciate or support him for who he was.

But as soon as Don moved down to the beach, he immediately became everything he most wanted to be. For him, it was high school all over again.

Amazingly, we found an old Dick Brewer '70s big-wave gun in somebody's trash in Venice. The fin had broken off and it needed some ding repair, but the moment it was fixed up and I had treated Don to a new wetsuit, he hit the waves. He soon figured out however, that a thick board meant for riding huge Hawaiian surf was not for the Venice breakwater!

But that Brewer board had an incredible history, which we later learned from the guy at Aqua Tech who had repaired it. It is something of a miracle that this particular guy recognized this board as the very same one he had worked on years before, at Brewer's shop in Hawaii! It had been custom-made for some mainland heir who lived in Malibu. How it ended up broken in the trash in Venice beach 20 years later, is a total mystery.

Life in our little nest was indeed growing old fast, however. There was my problematical history with the town, and even though it was all new to Don (who, before he moved in, had been living out at his Mom's close to Palm Springs in 100+ degree heat), we were both ready to move on. Like everything else that was coming together too perfectly, too fast, he had landed a really good day job working as a graphic artist at the Recycler, an advertising weekly that everybody in southern California had either bought once in their life or saw every day at the checkout stand. At 49 years old, he was going to go from having been a cut and paste artist, to immersing himself in the challenging new world of computer graphics. In the '70s, Don had been the Art Director at Hot Rod Magazine and had worked for such animated giants as Hanna- Barbera in the early-to-mid '80s. He was one talented dude.

Don had originated from Inglewood, just east of Westchester, where the rest of The Turtles had sprung from. Right down the road from Westchester High School, was the little coastal village of Playa Del Rey. The large expanse of beach that encompassed Playa Del Rey and nearby El Segundo (aka 'Mayberry by-the-Sea'), was called Dockweiler Beach ('D and W' to the surfers).

And it was there some 32 years earlier, that Don had learned to surf for the first time.

So it was eerie and amazing that life had taken him full circle when, in the summer of 1995, we moved into a modest one-bedroom loft apartment in Playa, just walking distance from the Westport Beach Club (now condominiums), where the pre-Turtle Crossfires had once performed. We would shop in a shopping center not far from where Don and the boys had bought their first instruments. He would drive me past places from his youth and bring me into a time that was, for him, the best moments of his life.

Except that year, when it all came together for Don Murray in one last fell swoop.

19

"so happy together...."

I was very surprised to find that the issue of whether the man I was with was politically correct or not, was a non-issue in this case. Not that my politics or my concern for social justice had changed. It's just that my priorities did. And having just come from barely surviving the major neurosis of two men, I was content on just having a decent, happy life without the drama for a change.

So when Don had told me that when he was very young, he basically had followed his family in supporting Barry Goldwater— after my initial horror, I lectured him briefly, let him know where I stood, then didn't bring it up again. I was tired. I needed to give it all a rest and take care of myself and let the world do the same. I had earned it.

Don hadn't seen Tom Stanton from The Crossfires since 1964. Don went on to form The Turtles with Al Nichol, and Tom went on to Vietnam.

One night in January, we were invited to a party on a gorgeous catamaran in Long Beach. A musician friend of Don's had invited another musician he sometimes jammed with. It turned out to be Tom Stanton! Now if ever there was an example of long lost brothers personified, they were it. They played together that night at the party and what sprung from that was a eureka that is still reverberating in some circles, to this day.

126

Don and I had just been turned onto a totally amazing instro band from San Francisco called The Mermen. They were a 3-headed monster that created a psychedelic sonic boom like nothing we had ever heard, except if you threw Jimi Hendrix, Pink Floyd and Dick Dale into a blender, that might be an accurate description. Theirs was an awe-inspiring array of sounds that basically reflected what a 30-foot wave might sound like, emanating from deep below. Don recognized that what this band was doing was the future of the surf genre—even though the trad purists would just as soon challenge us to virtual duals over whether The Mermen were truly 'surf' or not.

When Don excitedly turned Tom Stanton onto this band, it was the spark that ignited both of them to re-form The Crossfires, and launch their campaign to knock the music world on its ear. Probyn Gregory from L.A.'s power pop band, The Wondermints, was brought in on second guitar. Probyn now tours with Brian Wilson.

Don was still gigging with The Surfaris but for him, it had grown stale playing what amounted to an oldies revue for 15 years. He was actively seeking to hang out with and listen to the newer '3rd wave' surf bands, such as The Insect Surfers, The Halibuts and from Finland, Laika and the Cosmonauts.

Finally, The Mermen came to town, and it was so amusing seeing Don beaming over them and asking them to sign their latest CD at the time, *A Glorious Lethal Euphoria*. Truly profound was the artwork on the album cover, portraying a man seemingly engulfed in flame, and what seems to be a big cross held up in front of him. But even more profound was what two of The Mermen had written on the cover.

Guitarist Jim Thomas wrote: "To Don & Jamie, your cross+fire!" Allen Whitman, their bass player, had written: "To Don: full circle!"

That 4th of July, we had our first party at the new place and reveled in the fact that, from our roof, you could see spectacular fireworks really close, as they were shot from the Marina jetty. I watched them every year from that roof for the next 9 years.

The Crossfires practice sessions, which also began that July, were held in a small Hermosa Beach complex that also housed

Tom's surfboard shaping room. One night they actually played in his shaping stall! Next to Becker, Stanton boards were the bomb in Hermosa. There was something truly authentic about playing this kind of music, with the aroma of resin permeating everything, and the surfboard dust raining down from the rafters upon your head. I loved it. Don loved it. Life was perfect. So perfect that Elliot Easton of The Cars heard the new Crossfires, and even from a very rough practice tape, decided he'd be honored to produce their first CD!

Yes, life was perfect that year. There was our new regimen of surfing together in the early morning, or toward sunset at what we called 'golden diamond time'. There was the transformation of our new home into the 'Enchanted Tiki Pad' with shells and fish nets, tikis and Hawaiiana everywhere. There were long hikes in the sage-scented hills above Malibu and camping on the beach near Point Magu where at night, the ocean melted into the stars and, just like another place of beloved memory, it seemed like one giant velvet painting. There were nights at home, happily cuddled up with a video. And those days every month when we would search the comic book shops furtively, for the latest X-Files comic from Topps.

And there were friends, lots of friends that usually came in pairs, like us. Not even with Sandy, did I have a consistent community of other couples around me.

And for the first time in my life, I was not waiting for anything. I was not waiting for success, nor was I waiting for a person, place or thing. I had no agenda, no pressing need to do or be anything. I was completely content and at peace with myself and everything about my life.

For me, the once radical lesbian feminist, who would never even allow a man to open a door for me, it had to have taken one helluva man to get me to wake up in the morning actually looking forward to making his breakfast, lunch *and* dinner. I had only ever seriously entertained those kind of domestic fantasies with Gene.

I adored having someone who adored me. There were no agonizing what-ifs running through my head anymore. I wasn't having to play second fiddle to anyone else either.

Don appreciated and validated me in every way; my thoughts and feelings, the way I looked, the things I enjoyed, my past, my talents, my friends and my family. Totally the opposite of Phil. And Gene hadn't been ready to manifest that in a day to day reality. I was so glad that finally, my mother got to see me happy for a change.

She told me in the beginning, "He doesn't have a pot to piss in—but he adores you." She, of all people, had learned the value of that.

On a sweet August evening, nearly a year to the day that we met, Don and I returned to the old wooden planks of the Santa Monica Pier. The Shirelles were playing that night and there was a fence surrounding the backstage area, just like there had been a year before. Don asked the security guard if he could stand on the other side just for a moment—to be exactly where he had been when he first saw me.

And there, through the fence—we kissed. It was truly the most romantic thing that had ever happened to me.

One of the first gifts that Don had ever bought me, was for my birthday in November of '94 (only 6 days apart from his). It was a big Pooh bear wrapped in purple Pooh paper. I realized with astonishment, that this was a very rare individual who paid such great attention to detail and took such great care—because in only having seriously known me a month, he took a mental note that I loved Pooh and that purple was my favorite color!

Of course, I would turn around and do the very same thing.

Don had been videotaping and collecting all the episodes of *Mystery Science Theatre 3000*, a cable show that I had never seen, until Don invited me into the portals of Deep 13 (where a lot of the show takes place). I wrote to the fan club and got him some stickers and pictures, and finally, a really luxurious *MST3K* sweatshirt, the Christmas of 1995.

It was to be our last Christmas.

20

"I am the god of hell fire, and I bring you....."

Had I known that those precious months between October '94 and December '95 would be the best months of my life, I would have savored every moment, every precious waking moment of every day. How true the adage that one does not truly appreciate something until it is gone.

Just days after that tryst on the Pier, I got a call from Don's office that he had fainted at work and had been rushed to Lakewood Hospital. I frantically made my way there, to find him lying in a bed with a tube down his nose, and what seemed like blood being pumped out. What I later learned was that it was a bleeding ulcer. He then told me he once had ulcer problems and had surgery some years before. And even though he had still been smoking, his new lifestyle surely would have contributed more to a feeling of contentment, rather than churning stress. I just didn't understand.

What I didn't know was that Don had been in a lot of pain (sound familiar?), popping aspirins like candy—like Gene used to do. And once again, I was oblivious. Turns out there was more to Don's happy-go-lucky cool surfer dude facade than he would let anyone see. He may have looked like Doonesbury's Zonker character, but that was on the outside. And much like Gene's hidden rage, there were years of rage built up *inside* Don, and a lot of it had to do with his first marriage, the loss of his kids and what he felt was a betrayal from his brothers, the other Turtles.

Oh my god, hadn't I been through this movie before? Wait.

When Don would tell me his stories of The Turtles, how he left the band at the height of their success in 1966, probably only within weeks or months of Gene leaving The Byrds, I held my tongue and didn't say a word. I never told Don about Gene. I thought it would have looked really bad, like I was some kind of groupie.

The Byrds and The Turtles were like mirror images caught up in that particular time, that very *same* time, both bands having broken onto the charts with Dylan songs. And even though Don wasn't in the band any longer by 1968, The Turtles had their very last hit that year with a song called "You Showed Me", which was written by—Gene Clark! I just couldn't go there. It was bad enough I had to apologize for my relationship with Sloan, also a shard of that same cosmic mirror.

The next few months were a flurry of life-affirming activities and blind denial. Though Don stopped smoking right then and there, he refused to let anything alter his new way of life.

The very next month in September, we met up with Tom Stanton down in Carlsbad, and Don rode the brand new custom-made 8' 8" Surfaris board that Tom had made for him. On September 29th, Don played his very last gig with the Surfaris, at an outdoor festival in Diamond Bar.

There was the surf meet at Doheny Beach in Dana Point that October. We surfed all afternoon while our new friends, The Eliminators, played from the beach. Somebody took a video of us dancing and Don looked like he was in a state of bliss, his face turned upward toward the sun, eyes closed, dancing his happy 'bear dance'.

Don met my brother Denny that month, at one of my brother's gigs at the Ice House in Pasadena. Denny is a comedian and musician (the one still gigging off and on with the New Christy Minstrels) and his name is actually to be found etched onto the front window of the famous Comedy Club on Sunset, which was once Ciro's, where The Byrds got their start (6 degrees).

My father had even met Don, on a brief trip through the city earlier that May. What my father said to me without any reservation was stunning.

"Marry him."

That November, Don and I hosted a crew of friends over at the Tiki Pad for his 50th birthday. Besides Tom Stanton, the crew included his old Turtle mate and original bass player, Chuck Portz. Later a group of us went to Magic Mountain, where Don got to show off his bravado on every roller coaster the place had to offer. He and Tom went on the Free Fall while I stood down below, petrified.

There were the enhanced familial gatherings for the holidays. I say enhanced because, where once I would show up alone feeling like a total loser, now I had Don by my side. I was a real validated person with a real validated life. That wonderful feeling again of not waiting for anything.

Then the results of Don's upper G.I. test came back, and he was told that he had to have surgery to remove the source of the blockage that was making it difficult for him to digest anything. There was scar tissue from the previous surgery and it had to go. We were reassured that what sounded like a very complicated and impossible procedure, was actually quite common.

They would be cutting off the bottom end of his intestine and re-attaching it to his stomach (nearly the identical surgery Gene had in 1988!). The surgery was scheduled for January 3, 1996. That gave us Christmas and New Year's at least to enjoy, before our leap into the unknown.

Remember those key words earlier? Here they are again: ulcer—and surgery.

The Cosmic Ranger flipped a coin. It was neither heads nor tails.

The last Crossfires practice was held on November 26th, Christmas came and went, and we held our last party at the Tiki Pad on New Year's Eve.

On New Year's day, Don and I went surfing at El Porto in Manhattan Beach for the last time. We savored every wave, because we didn't know how long it would be before he could once again paddle out on his board. Abdominal surgery, he said, was one of the worst for pain. It could be a long while.

So on the morning of January 3rd, 1996, Don and I walked in together to Santa Monica- UCLA Hospital.

The initial surgery took 3 hours and was seemingly successful. Don was a little dopey from the medication but otherwise okay, enough for me to be able to go home and sleep that night. The next day, he was still in the intensive surgical unit but was to be moved up to his room that day. I stayed in his new room with him that night, long after visiting hours were over, curled up at the bottom of his bed. He was talking and everything. He seemed fine. I went home.

At 10 a.m. the next morning, his doctor called as I was getting ready to leave for the hospital. He told me Don had gotten very ill overnight and he was now in the critical care unit.

My heart went into my mouth. I fled to the hospital. They let me in only for a moment. He was breathing really hard. They told me that he would have to be put on a ventilator.

It—all—happened—so—fast.

I never heard his voice again.

On the 6th of January, 3 days after Don had entered the hospital, I got word from Florida that my Dad had died. I didn't even have time to grieve.

For the next 80 days, just short of 3 months, I never left the hospital, except to take a shower or pick up the mail. I slept there *every* night. Don had 3 more surgeries in an effort to stem the sepsis that was slowing killing him.

He never went home again.

21

"I'm gonna leave this city, got to get away"

Nineteen months—that's all Don and I had. Nearly the exact amount of time together that Gene and I had spent apart, while I was waiting for him to come back for me. What kind of cruel cosmic joke was this? What was my horrible karma that now, I had a beautiful ring and a promise left unfulfilled from one man that was dead, and a marriage proposal from another who had just died? And both of them died basically of complications from the same thing!

We held the paddle out ceremony for Don the morning of April 22ⁿᵈ, 1996, at our local break, El Porto. I was so physically distraught and exhausted, that I couldn't make it past the shore break. So I stood helplessly on the shore, and watched as a pod of dolphins circled around the mourners three times and swam on.

Later that day, the benefit concert posthumously held for Don, called *A Surfer's Paradise,* and organized by his friends Tom Stanton and Paul Johnson ("Mr. Moto"), brought together the biggest multi-generational group of surf bands the genre has ever seen. It is still the Woodstock of surf shows.

If you were fortunate enough to have been there, you would never forget it. Just about every who's who of reverb was there at the old Strand in Redondo Beach, with the exception of Dick Dale.

Going all the way back to the early '60s with: The Surfaris, The Chantays, The Lively Ones, The Tornadoes, and The Bel Airs, to mid-60s band, Davie Allan and The Arrows.

Then came the next class of guys who appeared in the late'70s into the'80s: Jon and The Nightriders, The Packards, and Thom Starr and The Galaxies.

What is called the Third Wave, was most inspiring, because this was the music that Don was so stoked about, as he was always looking forward. These bands were: The Halibuts, The Eliminators, The Insect Surfers, and The Surf Kings (which was the new name for Tom Stanton's band, now that The Crossfires would sadly, have to be retired).

Finally the coup de grace, driving all the way from Denver where they had been on tour—Don's beloved Mermen.

I have all 10 hours of the show on VHS.

All of the original surviving Turtles showed up for *A Surfer's Paradise*—with the exception of the two most obvious: Flo and Eddie, aka Mark Volman and Howard Kaylan. I knew that Howard was living out of state at the time, so I cut him some slack. Al Nichol came in from Carson City, Nevada, and Jim Tucker, from Grass Valley in northern California. And yes, Chuck Portz was there too.

But Volman still lived in Westchester, only a few miles away from Redondo Beach, and he had just gotten back into town. I knew that because I had spoken to him on the phone.

I will never forget that.

When Sloan played the 'comeback show' at the Troubadour, Flo and Eddie were listed on the bill. Mark Volman decided he didn't want to endorse the show or something, and threatened to sue if his name wasn't taken off the bill.

I never forgot that either.

Through the years, the extended family of Don's friends and fans, became the glue that held me together. They are still a big part of my life, and I *owe* them my life. It wouldn't be the last time however that a group of virtual strangers would surround me with love and support, at a crossroads that would nearly take me down .

One of the last things I promised Don in the hospital, when he was still coherent enough to understand, was that I would carry his name one day. I was referring to the fact that he had, indeed, asked me to marry him. We never got that chance.

And so, in March of 1996, I adopted an additional persona: Jamie Murray. And there are an entire group of people that only know me by that name and know nothing of my past.

For the next 8 years, in the apartment in Playa Del Rey, I never even moved Don's tooth brush. I was locked in a time warp, shell shocked and numb. I kept my sanity by working at my new found gig as a sales rep in the surf industry. That and surfing pretty much saved my life.

Don had started his own graphics company in early '95 called Mach Turtle Productions. He couldn't escape The Turtles, just as Gene would have bands with 'byrd' in the name. I decided to keep Mach Turtle alive and carry it on for my business, which was what Don would have wanted because it was about surfing, eventually encompassing surf music as well. I started distributing a line of CDs, small at first, but it grew to about 40 titles, including Don's favorite band, The Mermen. I became the exclusive one-stop where the surf shops and smaller record stores could get the stuff, before the downloading phenomenon eventually made it all disappear.

I even got into the band booking business, providing Southern California's indigenous music for event companies, who wanted an authentic sound to let their corporate masters know exactly where they were.

That turned into a six-year gig at a well-known Mexican restaurant in Marina Del Rey, the Baja Cantina. I brought them every manner of surf and instro band available, even some foreign bands that were touring the States. Wednesday nights at the Baja are still being talked about by those who were lucky enough to have been part of that scene. Peter Tork from the Monkees even showed up one night to jam with one of the bands! *That* was a total surprise.

My best friend Dena moved in a couple years after Don died, taking our bedroom upstairs, while I stayed down in the living room on a futon. It was too hard for me to sleep in that bed anymore.

I became a road warrior sales rep, hitting the road to sell my lines, whether they be bodyboards, sandals, CDs or trinkets from Hawaii. I went as far south as San Diego and as far north as Bodega Bay. I would sleep in the back of my Honda CR-V and surf different spots all up and down the coast.

As the California rep for Mauna Kai Hawaii, an accessory company out of Maui, I was privileged to be an insider in the surf industry for years, participating in many of the trade shows, where I would meet the legends of surfing: Mike Doyle, Greg Noll, Corky Carroll, Robert August, Rabbit Kekai, Laird Hamilton and Jeff Clark to name a few.

I never got to meet the beautiful and inspirational water woman, Rell Sunn of Makaha, but her daughter Jan sold me the vintage-style Hawaiian bamboo furniture that is the centerpiece of my living room today.

I also used my job as an excuse to drive up to the Bay area to see The Mermen, who by then had become my new Grateful Dead. In fact, their fan base was made up of many Deadheads, since they were apt to launch into long psychedelic jams. I loved it and could out dance and out spin just about anybody at their shows.

It was now the new millennium and with it, the G.W. Bush years. And how that started out for me was particularly memorable.

That November 2000 night, as the election returns were trickling in, I had this overall sense of dread. So I called the one person who I thought would understand; the one person I could talk politics with who wouldn't stare back at me blankly.

Sloan.

I went over to his house and we sat with bated breath through the excruciating process of election night. And as anyone who was there remembers, it was a roller coaster ride. When they called Florida for Gore, of course we were relieved. But then the unthinkable happened. There was a complete reversal of fortune, and the TV news channels called Florida for Bush.

It was at that point that Phil quietly got up, went into the kitchen—and promptly threw up in the kitchen sink!

That was one of the last times Phil and I got together as friends. How apropos, though.

Before Dubya ever walked into the White House, I was down at the Federal Building in Westwood, protesting the Bush v. Gore Supreme Court catastrophe. I spent the inauguration of Bush at an alternative event held in downtown L.A. called the 'Counter Inaugural', put on by an online group I helped to proliferate called Countercoup.

And marching with me, I had my new 8-year-old Australian shepherd Billie, who made all the difference in the world, as she became my traveling partner up and down the state.

The country was getting more politically oppressive and more factionalized and after the events of 9/11, it was starting to become dangerous to be a liberal critical thinker. From the beginning of the Iraq war onward, I would spend a good deal of time protesting the war, both in L.A. and San Francisco. I decided at some point that I wanted to be around more people like myself, free and critical thinkers (read: hippies). So, when the opportunity arose that a friend of mine up in Santa Rosa, who was playing percussion for The Aqua Velvets, offered to come down and take me and everything I own up to Sonoma county—I bailed outta L.A. like my ass was on fire.

I was finally able to move Don's toothbrush.

I kind of thought after 8 years, that maybe it was time to try a boyfriend kind of thing, but my new found friend John (another Scorpio), ended up being just that, a good friend.

I mostly lived pretty rough and rustic up there over the next few years, from living in an 18-foot travel trailer, to renting a room in Bodega Bay, to finally settling in a little cabin in the redwoods of Forestville. Billie hated it because the tall trees frightened her. By then, she was 13 years old.

Surfing up there was cold, gnarly and sharky. Every major shark attack on the U.S. mainland for the last 25 years, had mostly been centered around the 'Red Triangle', which is basically where I was. There were some spots I really enjoyed, like the hippie enclave of Bolinas in Marin county, where the residents move the street sign on the highway so you can't find the place, and where the infamous Suzy Creamcheese was supposed to be living. I'd hear things out in the water like, "Oh man, you shoulda seen the big one here yesterday. Swam right under my board. Dude, it musta been 15 feet!"

Then there were the days that I would sit huddled upon craggy, wind-swept hills, overlooking the ocean on the Sonoma coast—and I would think of my beloved Gene. He had looked at much the same scenery 30 years earlier. Mendocino was just the next county up. How cruel, the fates. So very close—yet, a lifetime away. How different our lives would have been, had we kept driving north and run away together.

Gene would probably still be alive.

I wouldn't have wasted 9 years with Phil, who was emotionally unavailable. I would have never met Don, true. But I also wouldn't have had to see him die in my arms.

As soon as I would think of Gene, I would brace against the wind, swallow my tears and drive quickly away. It was all too painful and I had buried it for so long. I dared not face that, another dream that was literally dead.

No one up there knew anything of me and my past. I was invisible yet again. I was biding my time. There was no urgency to wait for anything because there was no longer anything I wanted. I was an empty canvas, open to be painted upon, but with a dry palette.

At the end of October 2006, I got word that my friend Jo Jo Laine had died in London. It was impossible to imagine that vibrant, beautiful woman, who was only a year older than me, was now gone. She became another one of the litany of friends who would have their lives ruined by alcohol. She had been diagnosed with liver failure right before her death, which oddly enough, was not how she died.

Jo Jo had suffered a fatal fall, hitting her head while visiting the most cherished place of her life, the house at Yew Corner in Middlesex, which had been the house A.A. Milne used as his inspiration for the Winnie the Pooh books. Jo Jo and Denny had bought and lived in the house in the '70s, and Jo Jo had always said she wanted to die there.

She got her final wish.

My mother had the bright idea of me getting my real estate license online, because somebody she knew had done it. I only knew that I had avoided that business all my life. My mother had been a heavy hitter for over 40 years in Beverly Hills real estate, selling to high profile celebrities, and I was just not of that ilk, it was not my world. But this was Sonoma county, where real estate agents looked more like curio shop owners, and where many of the houses could be run-down farms or commune material. That was more my speed. It was a semi-rural area, not a big bustling city. I could hang with that.

And so I did. I got my license on the first try. I joined a little outfit in the town of Sebastopol, and sold a $750,000 house to Dick Dale's old bass player, Ron Eglit—before the company dumped my ass. There really wasn't anything left to hang around for. My friends, my elderly parents, the relatively warmer ocean— all were calling me back. So I packed up my little cabin in the redwoods, and went home to L.A., "city of the doomed" ("Los Angeles" - Gene Clark).

❝❞

"remember, life is never as it seems—dream"

She made it to 15, my beautiful Billie girl. But she never got to see 2008. She missed it by one day, having gone to the Rainbow Bridge at 12:31 PM on 12/31, New Year's Eve day of 2007.

We had driven down from Forestville to spend Christmas down in L.A., and we were staying with Dena, who had bought herself a little mobile home. Billie just wanted to die at 'home', to be with the two people she had loved the most.

When I returned back up north, with the exception of the Steller's jays and the acorn woodpeckers fighting over the peanut feeder, the silence in that cabin was deafening. The loneliness was unbearable. I could not be without the comforting sounds of a dog for very long, so I started looking at the NorCal Aussie Rescue website, where I saw a little boy named Chico, a blue merle with a full tail just like Billie.

His sweet little face stayed with me the entire time I was in Maui.

I had been working for Mauna Kai Hawaii for 10 years by then, and amazingly, had never been to Maui. Why? Because I would never leave Billie. I had learned my lesson from when I had left poor Gypsy for a year and a half. So when Billie died, I went on my 'broken- hearted Maui tour.'

At the same time, I kept an eye on Chico's status over on the rescue website. The rescue group's policy was that they didn't hold dogs on reserve, and so I was on pins and needles waiting to see whether I could get him in time. I had competition. There was an agility performance group that had their eye on him too, because the rap on Chico, was that he could scale a six-foot fence standing still. Luckily, they ran out of time to evaluate him and so, as soon as I got back to the mainland, I was driving up to Grass Valley to get him.

When I relocated back to L.A. in May of 2008, Chico was embarking on his new life as a spoiled SoCal beach dog.

As I was getting ready to drive back home to L.A., I decided to look up my old friend Rabbi David Montag, to let him know I was coming back home. I was shocked to learn that he had passed away only a couple months before.

I found myself once again feeling cut adrift, not knowing where I belonged or what to do with myself. How many times had this happened in my life when returning to this town?

I took a small apartment in a friend of a friend's house, but that got old real fast. My family decided it might be time for them to help me get a place of my own, just a condo or something reasonably affordable—for my twilight years. I then remembered the funky mobile home park across from where I used to surf at Sunset Beach in Pacific Palisades. I thought surely there would be no way there could be a place available to buy there, since once people got in, they rarely left. But lo and behold, we got lucky, and for the first time in my life, I became an actual homeowner (well, you own the house, but not the land under it).

It took a couple years and slowly but surely, I was re-assembling the scattered parts of my life, all under one roof. It was also really cool to have one of my favorite surf spots literally right across the street. That's if I felt like taking my life in my hands crossing Pacific Coast Highway on any given day to get there.

In June of 2010, I lost my beloved step-father Jack Wells, who, even though he married my mother in 1972, had been my Dad essentially since I was 14 years old.

Jack had been a well-known popular radio and TV personality in his hometown of Baltimore. When he moved to L.A. in the early '60s, he found plenty of work in everything from radio to TV to voice-overs. He had a deep, booming, instantly recognizable voice when he walked into a room, and he was loved by everyone who ever came into contact with him. His positive attitude was infectious, and even though we were worlds apart politically and culturally, he was one of the biggest champions I've ever had in my life.

Back at the new enchanted tiki pad, I had no grandiose plan, no sudden flourishing social life, and no desire to do much of anything except work at what I could, enjoy my new dog and life at the beach. I had no unfinished business that I knew of—until May of 2011, when the Cosmic Ranger sent me a rather painful reminder in the form of—the sciatica from hell.

I thought the pain that radiated down from my butt all the way to my right foot, crippling me, was aggravated by my digging out from a rain-induced flood that had brought mud and rock down from the hillside behind my house, a couple months previously. But the timing of this affliction was particularly suspect. It was only a couple months later, when my well-intentioned friend Laura started innocently sending me old Byrds videos from You Tube (along with the Buffalo Springfield, who had re-united for a tour), that it would lead me dangerously to further explorations.

Finally, there I was, face to face again, albeit on a computer screen—with Gene Clark.

Ever so faintly came the sound of a striking match.

The realization hit me with a staggering heart-bomb, that it had been the 20th anniversary of his death. I had never dealt with my grief, my anger, or the questions surrounding that dark day back in 1991, when I lost the first man I had ever truly loved. It all came crashing down upon me like a 30-foot three-wave hold-down at Mavericks. I couldn't even come up for air.

Then there was the fact that I couldn't talk to anyone about it, because it had been locked away in the vault of my heart that I dared not open for 20 years. To have to explain what was certainly a form of post-traumatic stress, was adding to my overwhelming desolation. It is a common misnomer, that this condition only happens to victims of war. But there are all kinds of wars, and the wounds of the heart are sometimes the hardest to recognize.

Lee Strasberg had said, "Our experiences are literally engraved in the nervous system. They are woven into the fabric of our existence, and can be relived, though we usually don't like these things awakened." Literally engraved in the nervous system— which is perhaps why I now have permanent nerve damage from that emotionally charged bout of sciatica. But Strasberg's teachings would also come into practice when it was necessary for me to finally access that sealed vault of my heart.

I had been very good over the years at burying everything, and at keeping Gene's confidences, even in the face of something as obvious as having gone with Laura months earlier to see Roger McGuinn live on a bill with Joan Baez. This is what prompted her to send me all those Byrds videos in the ensuing weeks. You would think it would have been an opportune moment to finally deal with all that pain and tell somebody.

But if my Method acting training had taught me one thing, it was to be able to envelop myself so completely in an emotional memory, it put me literally into another place and time. So at that very moment, in my head, I was just an eleven year-old kid, back in the kitchen of the old house in Benedict Canyon, wearing my Byrd glasses and watching The Byrds on a little black and white TV, back in 1965. I had to be. It was the only way to cope.

That handsome guy with the tambourine? Oh yeah—him.

What followed for several months was an intense and emotionally tormenting regimen, not unlike the exhausting game of catch up Gene and I had played so often. I spent hours on You Tube watching every video of him I could find, reading articles and websites, doing all the things that I had avoided for so many years, once access to a computer became commonplace. It was tortuous. I discovered that indeed, Gene had not been forgotten, that there were people out there in the world that were still talking about him and keeping his music alive.

I bought CDs that I had never seen or heard of, most of them issued after his death.

And that was when I discovered one of the songs he had written about us, "Your Fire Burning", the most heartbreaking of all.

The song was recorded from a live show with Carla Olson at McCabe's, just three months after I had last seen him. Where the hell was *I*? Where the hell was *he* that he didn't think to ask me to come to that show? What had been going on then? I ransacked my brain to remember.

I innocently put the CD on in the car, and when I started hearing his words, the very same last words he had spoken to me under that streetlight, I swerved over to the side of the road and nearly hit a parked car. I was devastated to the core. I had no idea.

Once my shock and anger subsided, there was only the haunting reality of my sweet Gene, laying his heart and soul out, stripped bare for everyone to see and hear. I was stunned, I couldn't believe it, hearing this ghostly recording from 1990. I have only ever listened to the song one other time. It was just too heartbreaking.

But I printed out the lyrics.

Then came the John Einarson book, *Mr. Tambourine Man,* and with it, so many of the excruciating blanks started to fill in.

It was pretty apparent that in those last 18 months, Gene went into a major downward spiral, once he had gotten that huge lump of royalty money from the Tom Petty recording. I had witnessed the beginning stages of it that last night, and it just got steadily worse from there. With his newly pocketed cash, and surrounded by the leeches who were intent on bleeding him dry, Gene could once again afford massive quantities of his substances of choice. From there, they say he went on to freebasing and heroin!

Is this the same sweet man who had dreams of taking me with him back to the woods of Mendocino? The person I was reading about bore only a passing resemblance to the man I knew. The master illusionist, most of the time he presented a whole other Gene to me. I had seen him in really bad shape many times, but I still couldn't believe what I was reading. It was like finding out that your favorite kindergarten teacher turned out to be a serial killer. Who was this person who did all that? And how did he deteriorate so drastically to that point?

I started to run it back, over and over in my mind, of what we had said and done, especially that last night. Did he, in fact, in his thoroughly inebriated haze, think I was leaving him? There were confusing lyrics in the song he had written about that night, as if to say he was losing me. Is that why he stood there silently watching me, as I innocently walked back to my car just a few blocks away? I had told him I loved him, as I buttoned his shirt up to protect him from the chilly autumn night. Surely he heard me say that.

What drove Gene to do what he did? Perhaps it had nothing to do with me. None of it made sense. But then it got worse still as I read on.

Sometime after the January 16, 1991 induction of The Byrds into the Rock and Roll Hall of Fame (which, adding to my ire, I learned that the old girlfriend had accompanied Gene on that trip), there was a shocking diagnosis of possible throat cancer, that was most likely the culminating factor that sent Gene totally over the edge and into the abyss. I instantly knew then in my heart, that he might not have wanted to live if he felt he couldn't sing. His voice was the mirror to his soul.

His desperation was also compounded by the fact that he could not go home again, to face his parents for their much anticipated 50th anniversary party, which was to take place literally the *next* day! His entire family was there waiting for him to show. He must have been so broken and ashamed, and perhaps the guilt literally must have made him want to die.

How could he not have let me or someone who truly loved him take care of him through all of that? Where was the number in his wallet that he could always call? Someone who would always listen? It was apparent that he didn't want anyone close to him around, because he relegated his fate to whoever showed up at his house.

The last month before he died, painfully thin and weakened, he soldiered bravely on and made one last tragic club appearance, in a 5-night stint at the Cinegrill on Hollywood Blvd. (lovingly referred to by his fans as 'Gene's last stand'). I had no idea about that gig and I guess it's a good thing. People who were there pretty much related that it was painfully obvious, that it spelled the end for Gene and his troubled, but prolific career.

From all accounts by people who witnessed what he was horrifically doing to himself those last few months, when the money ran out and he could no longer afford drugs, he basically seemed to have gone on a calculated suicide mission to drink himself to death. What little of his stomach that remained after the surgery, was just not enough to handle the onslaught.

Those last few days of Gene's life, as he slept on his own couch and alternated between marathon drinking and vomiting into a bowl, he was surrounded not by those who knew him and loved him—but by virtual strangers who showed up in his life, as if on cue, to feast on the carrion.

It's the oldest Hollywood story in the book. Gene died alone.

He ended up making that final sacrifice, to make sure he would not take those he loved most down with him. And he had warned me, yes he did. So many times. In a poetic way, as only Gene could, his martyrdom of a solitary death, may very well have been an act of love and pride.

And as I laid helplessly on the floor next to my bed in the hours following the news of his death, there at his house, the callous and vindictive girlfriend, along with her mother and brother, pillaged his home of everything that wasn't nailed down. By the time Gene's brothers David and Rick arrived on the scene from Kansas City, there was nothing left. Apparently Saul Davis had tried to protect Gene's guitars, but his meticulously handwritten notebooks of lyrics, his tapes, his clothes and most of his personal belongings totally disappeared, even as Gene still laid dead on the floor.

As of this writing, his Rock and Roll Hall of Fame award has still not been recovered.

Gene was finally taken home and buried in the place of his birth in Tipton, Missouri. He was a gifted and breathtaking poet, who set those poems free to fly through extraordinary song. Decades later, his music is still revered, and as it is so often through the ages, people who weren't even born during his lifetime, are now discovering him.

Somehow in the end, when he was beyond hope, with a broken body and soul, he lost sight of his very last dream. A beautiful dream that I believed would come true.

But he loved me as best he could, and protected me to the very end. I have to believe that.

And I will truly love him for the rest of my life.

23

"to everything, turn, turn turn—
there is a season...."

I needed to understand the significance of why a particular period of my life was literally coming back to haunt me 20 years later. How did it tie things up? What was the karmic lesson? How could I carry that forward and did it in fact tie things up at all? Or did it just lead to more questions and pain? I loathe the word 'closure'. It's so trite. That's not really what I was looking for. I needed a more consummate answer, something I could call on when the grief overtook me, something to hold on to when the questions and the frighteningly vivid dreams kept my mind swirling madly into all hours of the night.

The timing of the first ever Gene Clark Symposium, to be held in Overland Park, Kansas in the first week of November 2011, had to be more than just a coincidence. It was the Cosmic Ranger galloping by with a sneer, riding a phantom horse that had to have been saddled up that morning by Gene himself. It couldn't have been more weird. I felt like I was being manipulated by the cosmos at every instance. Too many times a Byrds song would be playing in the various sound systems at several stores I walked into. *Too* many times. Everything took on major significance as the time approached for this event to take place.

149

As crazy as it sounded, I found myself booking the hotel room where the symposium was to be held, and making plans to drive Gene-style half way across the country. His fear of flying was legendary. It was often cited as the reason he left The Byrds (there was a lot more to it than that). Surely I could honor him in this rather symbolic way (though knowing Gene, he probably would have chosen to take the train).

I told my mother I was going to the Grand Canyon for my birthday. I didn't want her to worry. Kansas City, my father's stomping grounds, really *was* half way across the country. And I couldn't explain where I was going and why to my mother in a million years.

So Chico and I, and my friend Laura (who I finally had brought up to speed on my past), packed up my Toyota RAV4, and hit the road for the most painful pilgrimage of my life. I dreaded that Gene's grave in Missouri lay at the end of that road and would be my final destination. It was the journey I dared not make back in 1991, when no one in Gene's circle or family knew of me, and I had to swallow my pride and stay silent. That would now have to change. It was time.

Gene's family had to know everything. They had to know that it wasn't supposed to end like that, that Gene had an alternate plan that somehow he didn't have the belief or the strength to attain. I knew that if they learned that he had at least been *trying* to get out of the way of the runaway train that was heading his way, it might bring them some comfort.

I started to get to know the people behind the symposium, the Gene Clark aficionados that had been carrying his torch for years. They had traveled from all over the country (though we had come the furthest from California).

Once I finally reached Kansas, slowly but surely, I felt comfortable enough with a few of them, that my story rather painfully started to come out in dribbles and drabs. It was nearly impossible to hide my raw emotional state. Since they had read every book and article and expose' on Gene that had been written in the last 20 years, they were intrigued to learn that there was an entire 4 years of his personal life that had been completely hidden under the radar. Though, they actually seemed to know more than I did about the man who tried to show me only the best of who he was. It was rather disconcerting, but oddly comforting.

As grateful as I was to finally meet Gene's younger brother David and his older sister Bonnie (for Gene had spoken of his family only in little anecdotes), it was heart-wrenching for me. There was so much I needed to tell them but couldn't share there, in a conference room, where people gathered to listen to some of Gene's unreleased recordings. It may have been the time but not the place. I ended up having to write letters to them both.

For them, it had been 20 years of the normal processing of grief. For me, with this newly torn open scab that bled out profusely over everything, it was as if Gene had died just last week.

The hardest realization for those few that learned of our story, was that in hearing of Gene's final plans to get out of L.A. again, he could have essentially avoided what became his tragic path to self-destruction. They believed he would have lived and so do I, if he had left before he had gotten too sick.

The proof of that came in traversing the area that Gene had once called his 'Sherwood', a green, beautiful parkland area of Kansas City called Swope Park, where he and his brothers would run through the woods barefoot, and where Gene had told me of the creek where he would find 'mudpuppies'. When we finally drove through the area and I saw his creek, I was stunned to see that it looked nearly identical to the road off the 101 in northern California, as you start heading west towards Boonville in Mendocino county! It would have been the quicker road Gene would have taken if he had been driving up from San Francisco, to where he had been living in Albion all those years ago.

The sudden realization and significance of this just tore me to pieces. What Gene had only wanted to do was to follow the breadcrumbs back—to go home again. But he knew he never could.

The devastating journey out to St. Andrew's Cemetery in Tipton was the hardest road I've ever traveled. Once I managed to finally get out of the car at the brick-pillared entrance, I could barely stand, and then I could barely walk the relatively short distance to Gene's grave. I was the last one to go in, and I was grateful that our intimate group afforded me that space. Somehow they knew, even the ones who didn't know. It could have been that I was the only one there totally draped in black, embellished by what could only be described as a widow's shawl.

The visible pain and loss, it surely covered me like a shroud. I was no longer having to hide anything. And as I finally stepped out of the shadows into the light, I didn't care who bore witness.

Once I found where he lay, I went about the task of giving him the best sage ceremony a white girl could offer. There was a heavy wind that blew on that hill, and wouldn't you know that Gene's bundle of sage, it just kept on burning down to the very end.

Just like he had said—his fire would keep burning.

As I had given him on the very last night I saw him, there at his grave, I left a medicine bag I had made, and an unburned sage bundle with a feather attached. Sometime later, I made a new friend there, a Tipton local who told me he would bring to Gene, whatever I would care to send out from California. The depth of gratitude I have to the people that took care of me there in Kansas and Missouri, I cannot even adequately express. I suppose the passage of time will allow me that.

But I will leave them with this, to store away in their mental scrapbooks and heartfelt collections, and in their future words when they speak of him, the man that they so honor with time dedicated and reverence paid. This is the man they might not see in the books and articles, though they may have caught a glimpse of him through his songs, or just that rare twinkle in his eye.

I call it—Basic Gene 101: honest, kind, hardworking, funny, gentle, protective, passionate, spiritual, proud, stoic, strong, vulnerable, sad, deep, a dreamer, a poet—and a voice you can never forget.

Mrs. Stevenson wrote in my 1971 Fairfax High School yearbook: "Jamie: Somewhere underneath that crass exterior of yours, and your belligerence, and your hostility, and your ego, is a warm, sympathetic, talented person. I hope she comes out soon! We'll all be much happier ☺"

Well, Mrs. Stevenson—at least I learned to truly love.

Perhaps that was the lesson after all.

FADE OUT (2011)

"and in the end, the love you take, is equal to the love you make"

The snuffling, comforting sounds of the dog in a nearby room, the tinkling of multiple wind chimes in the ocean breeze, the chitter chattering of birds at the backyard feeders—these are the outside remnants of what is now my life. There are no human voices here, save what comes from the local TV morning news. There is only me. And I try not to talk to myself.

But on the inside—oh, what a realm. The feel of that shiny black vinyl disc, containing therein my entire universe; the adolescent assured glances of instant recognition from the soul mate who shared a vision and made it a reality; the voices of earthly angels who gifted me with their melancholy tunes, and shared with me their exquisite madness; the deliciously overpowering scent of a lover spent and the grateful memory of a heart that still beat strong— still alive, so very alive!

And though I try to remember only the beautiful majesty of what once was, the grief overwhelms me. I see the loss in every waking moment. They surround me wherever I go—these ghosts. They are in the places that are now my hallowed shrines—in the sunsets I see through younger eyes, frozen in another time. They are in every song that I can no longer hear because of the pain. Even the taste of salt water on my skin is no longer the comfort it once was.

Perhaps I must move on yet again to another place, to see if the ghosts will follow. Alas, I know they will. They always do.

So I must follow the breadcrumbs back, back to the beginning—to see where I've been, and to see where I might be going.

My 60's warriors that bore the wounds and scars from a life and time that I so aspired to, these boys that were my heroes when I was a child, for some of them, I became the salve to their wounds, for they knew I *knew*. I saw them revealed as they truly were and I understood. So many of them are gone now. Still, some have managed to survive and I watch them lovingly from afar to see how they fare. There are those I do not know, but for every one of them that falls, I feel a stab to the heart. They are my older brothers and they are the living testament to all that I am.

The 6 degrees of separation phenomenon continues unabated. It started with Birdie, my best surfing buddy, telling me she had just gotten a new job with High Moon Records, a new company out of New York. Wouldn't you know it, they were re-issuing some old album from— Gene Clark! Of all the people in L.A. to get this gig, I'm sorry, that's just *too* much.

The little house in Sherman Oaks and Gene's landlord's house next to it on the same property, were both torn down in 1995, sold for practically nothing after the Northridge earthquake. A huge two-story gated stucco McMansion has taken its place. It's just as well. Until recently, I had not driven by there in all those 20 years, nor to any of the special places Gene and I called our own.

But there is now a framed picture of him up above our little corner booth at Corky's, the old Lamplighter. I made sure of that.

I had gotten the address from my cousin Roxanne in Phoenix, of a house in Kansas City where my father's relatives had lived. We have pictures of Dad as a kid taken in front of Grandma Nellie's house. It was right in the center of the city, not far from the Missouri River. Try as I might, I couldn't find the house, but as I drove over the bridge spanning the river, I started to cry, at the profound grandiosity of it all.

Not only that, but Rox had found in one of her mother's diaries, some entries describing how she and her brother, my father, would play in the woods, in a place called—Swope Park.

I did get to bring, on my way back to California, some Missouri sage from a shop in Tipton, to scatter on the 9th hole of the Phoenix country club where my Dad had hit a hole in one, and where some of his ashes had been scattered. And though he had given me his blessing to marry Don, I never got to tell him about the Missouri boy that I had loved so long ago—but I think he knows.

I still surf and take a wave for Don whenever I can. The community of people that were there for me back in 1996 are still there for me today, and I am forever grateful. Don and I were only given a year and a half together in this life—but to them, I will always be Jamie Murray.

My old partner Sandy is now a transgendered man, living in a suburb outside Melbourne, Australia. He has a new life with a new partner and even has stepchildren. He doesn't play music or paint anymore, but he has a sweet, goofy yellow lab named Toby and he's happy.

Dena is still my best friend and I talk to her once or twice a week. She is my rock and my reality check. I still call her a hillbilly sometimes. She lets me get away with it, but just barely. She finally knows *all* of my secrets.

Laura accompanied me on the most difficult journey of my life and for that I will forever be grateful. She is the most generous and thoughtful person I know and she still writes actual letters to people. Besides we're related now. Her Aussie, the gorgeous silver Raven, is Chico's main squeeze.

Philip Sloan is pretty much where I left him last I looked. We remained friendly for a while and would talk occasionally. But it really was the last straw when he inexplicably un- friended me on Facebook for absolutely no reason.

I gotta draw the line somewhere.

CODA (2016)

'Be careful what you wish for'. We've all heard that cliché, right? Here's another one: 'You can't make this stuff up'. The media is fond of using that, especially when referring to something so crazy whack and impossible to wrap your mind around, such as Donald Trump becoming President, for example.

Both clichés were put into play shortly after I arrived back in California from Kansas City in November 2011.

It all started with something I coincidentally overheard while still back there at that Gene Clark symposium. Well, you *know* there's no 'coincidentally' with me. But there it was, as one of the fans happened to be enquiring of Gene's brother David, on the whereabouts and the welfare of the younger brother who had moved to California back in 1970, and had a front row seat to the long and winding road of Gene's life and death out west.

No one in the family knew Gene better than his brother Rick, who right out of high school, decided also to try his hand at some semblance of success, as a burgeoning singer- songwriter out in California. I had a vague memory of seeing Rick back then at a couple shows, but had never met him. Gene never introduced us and I certainly wouldn't have approached his younger and very attractive blond brother, as I had already done the math on that.

What David Clark said filled me with dread and every red flag went up. He basically hemmed and hawed around the questions, but I got the gist of what he was saying—that brother Rick was somewhere in northern California, in some kind of half-way house, but they didn't know where. He said that Rick was in some kind of trouble.

That was what was weighing heavily on my mind on the long drive back to L.A., and for a few months after that, I couldn't stop wondering what had happened to Rick Clark.

The events after that in February of 2012 are nothing short of miraculous. I had continued to reach out online to some of the fans I was getting to know through Facebook. One guy in particular stood out, in both knowledge of music and the culture surrounding it, and just in sheer intellect all around. So I gave him my phone number and we continued our online conversation by phone, for what turned into two hours.

It was when I had told him of my trip to Kansas City, and just what it was I had overheard, that he told me he had been a friend of Rick Clark's and had an old number for him. He said he would try to call to see what was happening. When my phone rang not long after that, I picked it up and said "Well, that didn't take very long, did it?"

It wasn't the guy I had been talking to for two hours. It was Rick!

His speaking voice was so similar to Gene's, it was totally unnerving. Yet, I could tell that he was in a weakened state and that it was difficult for him to talk for very long. Our mutual friend had explained to Rick who I was, but I still felt uneasy about going into too much detail. I mostly wanted to listen to him and have him tell me what he could about what had happened to him.

In a short time however, I gathered enough bits and pieces about his situation to lead me closer to making a major, life altering decision.

Rick had been languishing from place to place, since his wife had thrown him out of their house two years before. I didn't ask why. He had a major car accident in 2010 that left him with a broken neck and back problems. Then, just around the time I was traveling back from his own brother's grave, he had a fall down two flights of stairs that turned his left foot clear around, ripping tendons and leaving his foot completely immobile.

160

From what he was describing of the place that he had found himself in, it sounded like hell on earth, where he was so cold in his dark and tiny room, he had to bundle himself up in a jacket to go to sleep at 7:30 every night, because there was nothing else to do. He had a TV, but the facility would have charged him so much extra for cable, it just sat there unused. Basically he was in a boarding house for people in 'transition', placed there by unscrupulous social workers and populated with mentally ill and criminal elements. The more Rick told me, the more I knew what I had to do.

On the 24th of February, I arrived in Eureka, California, some 270 miles north of San Francisco, to take Gene's younger brother and everything he had left to his name, and bring him home with me.

Rick was waiting for me outside the place when I drove up and I practically ran to him. As I looked up into his heavily bearded and frightened face, with blessedly familiar blue eyes that just broke my heart, I started to cry. All those years of pain and loss that we both felt in that one moment, merged, and we became one being. I couldn't believe that here was someone who already shared an immense part of my heart.

And me being the one person to come and rescue him, to offer him safety and solace, reaching across the years like some phantom appearing from another time—well, his brother's spirit surely knew the one place Rick would be safe and cared for. I knew this had to be true because it was all too incredible otherwise.

Rick would be the first to tell you that if I hadn't gone to get him right then, he surely would have died. He was so sick from malnutrition, he must have had all of 130 pounds on his 6 foot emaciated frame. His skin was literally hanging loosely on his bones.

So the first thing I did was take him by the hand, and like two long lost souls, we strolled slowly down to a restaurant where I bought him dinner. There, we tried to fill in some of the blanks of so many years past, but it was impossible to even start. He was so shell shocked that I could see it was difficult for him to get the words out. So it was enough for me to just sit quietly and watch him eat.

Later, I couldn't stand the thought of having to leave him in that place for one more night, so we could pack the car the next day. I was just praying he wouldn't die before I could get him out of there. When we stayed overnight the next night in a Motel 6, I listened to him breathing and there was a horrible rattling in his chest. He joked about it being the 'Humboldt crud', but it was not funny. I couldn't get him out of that town fast enough.

At breakfast the next morning, I saw just how damaged he was when he was nodding off, his head hanging precariously low over a plate of pancakes. At that point, I didn't know the particulars, but I could clearly see he was over-medicated on something.

In time I heard his story; how he would be seeing various doctors for panic, anxiety and depression issues, and where he would sit in the waiting room as a parade of drug reps would come through, their briefcases loaded with the latest samples of Big Pharma's poisons. Rick had become just another low-income American guinea pig in our health system's irrational and criminal carousel of legally prescribed drug abuse. I would learn just how insidious these addictions could be.

I also learned that what I had witnessed with Gene was precisely these same issues, that he was most likely *not* bi-polar as some had suggested, but merely dealing with a panic and anxiety condition, with depression episodes thrown on top of that. When he drank or did drugs, it only enhanced those problems to the umpteenth degree.

As we finally made our way down the northern coast, my car loaded to the roof with what remained of Rick's belongings (he lost most of his most precious possessions in that car crash two years before), we edged closer and closer to the place that had once been just a dream for me—Mendocino.

It was where Rick had gone to when he left Kansas after high school (where he had been quite the acting and musical theatre star), and went to live with Gene at the house in Albion. The overpowering emotion I felt when we spent the next night with an old dear friend of theirs, at whose house, Gene's wedding had taken place back in 1971—it was totally surreal. Everything seemed to be moving in slow motion, as I took in the magnitude of where I was and with whom..

Later that night, as I watched and marveled at Rick, sick as he was, steadfastly building a fire in the wood stove, I knew I had made the right decision. I knew that if I had stripped away all the baggage and even all the unknowns I was facing with this man, that he would turn out to have many of the positive attributes that I had adored in his brother. Because they were all there, just under the surface. I could see them in the way he would speak (with a Missouri drawl even more pronounced than Gene's), and the value he placed in certain things.

You could say, their parents raised them right and it showed. He too, had that genuineness, humor and self-effacing charm that I found irresistible. But I also knew that came with a caveat.

Rick shared many of his brother's demons as I was to discover. That was the bad part of 'be careful what you wish for'. This time however, I was not going to look the other way, walking on egg shells. This time I would say something and let those chips fall where they may. In all the years that had passed, even with a new awareness of what had happened to Gene at the end, the guilt and anger that I felt at not being able to save his life, it never went away.

It never went away for Rick either, who told me that after Gene died, he spent years "at the bottom of a bottle."

So this was to be my new mission, to try and save Gene's brother now? Well, I had to hope I was up to it. There *had* to have been a rather profound reason he was sent my way—or I was sent his. I mean, what are the odds?

And so, Rick settled into my digs at the beach with Chico and I, and spent the next two years trying to get well. It was a long arduous undertaking, requiring most of my time. Since he had lost his driver's license after the accident, I had to take him to doctor's appointments just about weekly for a variety of ailments. One of the most serious was the fact that he had Hepatitis C, apparently from a long ago blood transfusion after another car accident. It was the reason why he had to stop doing construction work many years before (one of his better stories recounted how he started out as a carpenter in the '70s, apprenticing under Harrison Ford, who had not yet hit the big screen in *American Graffiti*).

By 2012, 'Obamacare' had just started to be implemented and miraculously, under Medi- Cal (California's version of government subsidized health care), Rick got the $85,000 cure approved! He is now Hepatitis free. Bit by bit, he started to rebuild his body and mind, but there had been so much damage done to both, it sometimes seemed an impossible task. His immune system was shot.

As I had done with Gene so many years before, I tried to just offer Rick a safe place to be. I told him the chair outside on the deck that faced the ocean view was his domain now, and sure enough, he would go out there and sit quietly.

One day he started feeding peanuts to the scrub jays that gathered on the fence. One in particular became his best buddy and Rick named him Baby Jay. He literally had the jay eating out of his hand and it became his daily life-affirming ritual.

I knew Rick was a singer-songwriter as well and when he finally got inspired, I heard him play and sing for the first time. I couldn't believe it. Truth be told, he had to stand in his brother's shadow all those years and it was a tragedy for him. He made a joke about it though and said he introduced himself once on stage, announcing, "Hi, I'm Livingston Taylor." Rough deal. Now he had turned 60 and time was of the essence in so many ways.

In the summer of 2014, I made the decision to sell the mobile home as I just couldn't afford to live there anymore. That, and between the constant traffic, noise, the entitled rich in their new Teslas, and the police helicopters overhead during the obligatory L.A. car pursuits, I couldn't stand it. I was no longer surfing much and I didn't have the time anymore to hit the road as a sales rep. Taking care of Rick, I needed to stay close to home.

Our first choice was to return back to northern California, to Sonoma or Mendocino county. After three trips up there looking for an affordable place to live, it proved impossible. All those people that could no longer afford the city were moving further north, so we were out of luck.

Then Rick remembered a little mountain town where he had spent some time over the years. A very good musician friend and ex-bandmate of his had already set up a life there in the mountains of Idyllwild, an alpine village some 5000 plus feet in elevation, above the Palm Springs desert.

To me, Idyllwild was a mythical town that I had only heard about. Driving past the off ramp on the I-10 heading east, you would never know it was up there, this magical place where there seemed to be an abundance of baby boomers like us in outright hippie regalia and proud of it. There were no streetlights nor parking meters, and the only helicopter you might hear overhead would be in search of a lost hiker. The area was known all over the world for its first rate hiking trails and mountain climbing. In fact, Idyllwild is one of the stops along the 2,659 mile long Pacific Crest Trail (known as the PCT). It travels the length of California from Mexico clear to the Canadian border.

Two miles or so outside of town in a little paradise called Pine Cove, another thousand feet or so higher up, we found ourselves that little knotty pine cabin in the woods that I had been dreaming of all these years. And yes, I finally got the wood stove.

This was the good part of 'Be careful what you wish for'.

We wake up to an array of mountain bird life nearly identical to what I had left in Forestville: the Steller's jays, the acorn woodpeckers, mountain chickadees and dark-eyed juncos. Chipmunks and squirrels catch the bird seed that makes it to the ground from the feeders. Bobcats and deer will cross our paths and coyotes sing us to sleep.

We found a mountain lion track in the snow once. Oh yes, it snows in the winter! It is impossible for me to believe, but I don't even miss the beach. I am quite the mountain woman now.

Gene is never too far away from us—watching, guiding. This was the life he saw for me so long ago. How did he know?

Rick and I have taken two trips together now, back to their home town. I am now part of the family that I once couldn't even approach for fear of rejection. It is a comfort to me, a consolation prize if you will.

In November of 2014, shortly after we moved to our cabin, we drove all the way back to Tipton, for Rick to perform in a concert honoring Gene on what would have been his 70th birthday. There was also another show held at Knucklehead's in Kansas City. But that wasn't all. Missouri governor Jay Nixon had officially declared in a proclamation, that from hence foreword, Gene's birthday on November 17th would be known as 'Gene Clark Day'.

It doesn't get any better than that.

A month later, on December 20th, I lost my mother Shirley, at the age of 90. She went the way she had planned, in her own time and in her own home. It is with a heavy heart that I write these words on Mother's Day.

When I had told Mom several years ago that I was writing my memoirs, she told me to make sure to tell her on the day it was published, so she could be out of town. My mother's sense of humor—what more can I say?

In the last year or so of her life, confined to a wheelchair in her bedroom, Mom started to relive better days, back when the world was her oyster and she had the attention of that world famous singer she never forgot. She would mention his name over and over, and have a very familiar faraway look in her eye.

I realized then, that my mother and I were not so different after all.

Philip Sloan passed away on November 15th, 2015, from a pancreatic cancer that he had only known about for a few weeks. I never got to say good-bye, though it seemed I had been saying good-bye for a long, long time. His sweet little house, the only one he'd ever got to own in his life, was also razed to the ground after his death.

Sir George Martin died at the age of 90, just in March of this year. My brother KC had called me wondering why I hadn't been calling into radio stations or wasn't being interviewed on the news. After all, he said, how many people could say they made a record with George Martin? Somehow the thought never occurred to me.

But later that day on Facebook, I gave a little eulogy for Sir George and pretty much blew my cover. Another secret I had held for years, that so many friends never even knew.

We try to live simply day to day, aware of the miracle that is our new life. We adopted a little brother for Chico, a Louisiana Catahoula Leopard Dog named Zydeco. I guess that means we're a real family now.

I cook in my crock pot and try to keep the house clean, a never-ending deluge of dust and dog hair. We watch *way* too much news, so frightening that it usually makes us want to cocoon even more than we already do. Rick still has an array of health problems but in the winter, he can get out there with the best of 'em and saw that firewood!

Sometimes, when I watch him getting his morning coffee, it is an eerie thing. I look at his tall silhouette from behind, as he stands facing the kitchen window, with those familiar broad shoulders, and the way his hair falls just so. He once told me that he and Gene were like twins, the dark and the light.

I still don't know how to feel about that.

Sometimes, he gets really depressed and can't pick up his guitar. But on those days he does, it's magical. Soon he will finally be getting into a proper studio to record the several decades' worth of songs that have been waiting to see the light of day. With Merle Haggard gone, somebody's gotta pick up the slack. Besides, Rick has his own fan club out there, people who take the time to encourage him along his path. I guess I'm one of them.

And though I thought I really did understand the quiet desperation of 'one day at a time'—now I really do. Life can turn on a dime. Nothing is set in stone except one's gravestone.

Rick tells people about how this angel came along and saved his life. As I look out the window during the days at the majestic trees that surround us or listen to the peaceful silence of the nights, I want him to know, for what it's worth—that it was he who saved *my* life.

The Cosmic Ranger hung his wise old hat upon the Tree of Life and unfurled his bedroll upon the infinite Cosmic Range.

"All in a day's work," he said.

LINER NOTES

As with any labor of love that one pours their heart and soul into, especially the definitive story of a relatively short human lifespan upon this Earth, the players on that stage are many and they all deserve some thanks. I am hoping that I can touch some of them here, for without them, I would disappear. As we all learned from the *Back to the Future* movies, change one character or event and it causes a major paradox, as you disappear from your own snapshot.

I'd like to thank Robin Hergot Potharst for reappearing in my life in 2015, after a very long silence. I didn't mention her in the book because when I started it back in 1998, she was absent from my life, but she was a huge part of it. She was my childhood friend, my Beatle buddy, and my partner in crime for many of my formative years. We had a lot of catching up to do. Thank you, Facebook.

To Dittany Lang and Cherry Trumbull, thanks for being the adults in the room, for taking such good care of my family through the years and for still being there for me.

To my brother KC, I love you dearly. You have done so much for me and without you, I never would have made it back to 'Ewok Land'.

To my brother Denny, my sisters Julie and Patti, thank you for sharing this journey with me, even though we never all lived under one roof.

To sister Jennifer, who I saw only once when I was 15, trust that we will find you again. And to our lost baby brother Jody, we will never forget you, little cowboy.

Dana, you were the mythical sister that only existed in an old newspaper clipping from the '50s, but you came true. How crazy and wonderful is that?

To Amanda Levant Carmel Kramer, my ex-sister-in-law who is and always will be my family. I miss the holidays with you and your beautiful smile. My mother adored you.

To my nephews David and Charlie Carmel, I will always be your hippie dippy auntie. ☺

To my niece Kristin and nephew Jordy, I am blown away by your talents. You do your lineage proud.

To my step-brother Glenn Wells, who let me borrow his father Jack to have as my own for 40 odd years. Much gratefulness. Keep it psychedelic, my brother.

To my cousin Roxane, who faced so much adversity with aplomb and grace. You inspired me to greet every day with joy, hope and gratefulness. You are the memory of all my father's people and I will love you always.

To cousin Robin, you are the link to all my mother's people and when I think of you, I see pink flamingos. ☺

To John Aaroe and Darrell Wallace, thank you for all the opportunities, wisdom and friendship you shared with my mother, Shirley. You put up with me as I tried to function in a business that I was raised in, but did not belong in. My mother was the queen of that ball, and I couldn't hold a candle to her.

To Jim Lauver, waiter extraordinaire, whose smiling face and hilarious anecdotes at the late, great Hamburger Hamlet, made for years of fond memories. You will always be one of the centerpieces of my life.

Wayne Kasper, my brother in Tipton, I can't thank you enough for keeping the memory of Gene Clark alive and for schlepping the bundles of sage that I send for his grave. May you always hit a hole in one.

Likewise, Indigo Mariana, for your tireless work on Gene's behalf, including your efforts to get him inducted into the Songwriters' Hall of Fame.

To Paul Kendall and Four Suns Productions, for all the dedication that gave us the stellar documentary *The Byrd Who Flew Alone*. It is so unfortunate that Rick Clark was too ill at the time to be interviewed because nobody knew Gene better.

To the legendary Henry Diltz, whose gift to me for this book can never be adequately re-paid. Just know that I am forever grateful.

Saul Davis and Carla Olson, thank you for your talents, your insightful patience and your friendship. Sorry I took so long.

To Tim and Pamela Richardson, the latter who wrote an homage to Gene that will stand the test of time through the ages, "Tipton's Vein of Silver". Pam, you *so* got him.

To Dan Torchia, thank you for showing me Swope Park for the first time.

Jennifer Murray Reynolds, I only wish your father had been able to see the woman you have become. He would be so proud of you. Likewise, nieces Angela and Helen.

To Susie Manners, who was the only one who really understood my day-to-day exasperation of trying to understand Philip Sloan. Thank goodness he called you to be there for him at the very end. You did the time, honey.

Paul Zollo, who himself has been down in the trenches with every manner of songwriter and has written two Bible-worthy volumes on their unique perspectives, I am so grateful for all your advice and insight.

To my partners in commerce along the road, who gave me the opportunities to make a living without having to sell my soul: Ben Severson, Pascal Benoist, Lisa Hetman, Glenn Shimizu, Donna Yost, Bobby and David Chang, Dan and Becky Humes, Tom Nilsen, Tori and Jake Schwaner, Udo Wahn, Lissa Ross, Art Bourasseau, Paul Borelli, Dave Wood, Steve Soest, David Arnson, Joe Kurkowski, Tom Stanton, David Pascal, Neil Norman, Ferenc Dobronyi, Matt Quilter, Jim Thomas, George Nauful, Miles Corbin,

Michael Lindner, Robert Rankin Walker, Henry Wimmer, Jim Bacchi, Martin Cilia and Jeff "Big Tikidude" Hanson.

And to all those who took me in through the years, feeding me or giving me a place to crash on my journey: June Cannon, Rick and Rowena Wallach, Dawn Frasier, Patrick Alden Moore, Dave Becker, Jeff 'Stretch' Riedle, Jennifer Burnes, Martyn Jones, Allen Whitman, Phil Dirt, Jeniblue Walker, Ann Schneider, John Jones, Annette Arnold, Marina Andriola, Kathy Hallinan, Marni and Chris Wroth, Vera Tabib, Whin Oppice, Chris Adams, Kent Adams, Philip O'Leno, Ken and Carla Canby, Julie Frakes. Frank Altobello and Barbara Czescik

To the GC crew, who continue to fly high above the clouds: Barbara Xakellis, Lora Stefanski, Catherine Henry, Peter Santaro, Cheryl 'Pinkie' Jennings, Peggy Hansen, Uwe Rayer and the lovely and talented Tom Sandford, aka 'The Clarkophile', who was the first to step forward and "believe in me".

And to Bill See of Divine Weeks, whose book, *33 Days*, inspired me to have the courage to wrap up my own journey on the written page and gave me the title for this book.

Finally, the ultimate Fickle Finger of Fate Award goes to Buddy Woodward, without whom, Rick and I would literally not be standing here.

NOTATIONS

Einarson, John. *Mr. Tambourine Man - The Life and Legacy of the Byrds' Gene Clark*. San Francisco: Backbeat Books, 2005

McParland, Stephen J.. *P.F. Sloan - Traveling Barefoot on a Rocky Road*. N.S.W., Australia: CMusic Books, 2000

Priore, Domenic. *Riot on Sunset Strip - Rock'n'Roll's Last Stand in Hollywood*. London: Jawbone Press, 2007

Hirsch, Foster. *A Method To Their Madness – The History of the Actors Studio*. New York: W.W. Norton & Co., 1984

RECORDS *

In My Room (Wilson/Usher) 1963
So You Want To Be A Rock 'n' Roll Star (McGuinn) 1967
For What It's Worth (Stills) 1966
Rebel Rebel (Bowie) 1974
Bookends Theme (Simon) 1968
59th St. Bridge Song (Feelin' Groovy) (Simon) 1966
Baby You're A Rich Man (Lennon/McCartney) 1967
Without You (Ham/Evans) 1970
San Francisco (Be Sure To Wear Flowers
In Your Hair) (Phillips) 1967
The End (Morrison) 1967
Mr. Tambourine Man (Dylan) 1965
Secret Agent Man (Sloan/Barri) 1966
Bend Me Shape Me (English/Weiss) 1966
Your Fire Burning (Clark) 1989/92
Power To The People (Lennon) 1971
Ballad of a Thin Man (Dylan) 1965
Surfin' Safari (Wilson/Love) 1962
Do You Believe in Magic (Sebastian) 1965
Happy Together (Bonner/Gordon) 1967
Fire (Brown/Crane/Finesilver/Ker) 1968
Going Up The Country (Wilson) 1968
Remember (Christmas) (Nilsson) 1972
Turn Turn Turn (Seeger/Ecclesiastes) 1962
The End (McCartney) 1969

ABOUT THE AUTHOR

Jamie Johnston was born and grew up in Los Angeles, living between the worlds of old and new Hollywood. Her father was actor and recording star Johnny Johnston, whose starring role in 1956's *Rock Around the Clock* made her a bona fide Rock and Roll baby with a pedigree.

In 1972, fresh out of high school, Jamie and her songwriting partner Sandy, known as The Skiffles, made quiet history by being signed to Beatles' producer George Martin, and released a single on The Beatles' first label, Parlaphone. They were one of the first female rock bands to get a major record deal, playing their own instruments and writing their own songs.

Jamie went on to study acting with the illustrious Lee Strasberg, appeared in several films and theatre productions and worked in voice-overs for years.

She now resides in the mountains of Idyllwild, CA.

Printed in the United States
By Bookmasters